Including Lower-achievers

in the

Literacy Hour

Using stories and poems

Collette Drifte

HOPSCOTCH
EDUCATIONAL PUBLISHING

Contents

Published by
Hopscotch Educational Publishing Ltd,
29 Waterloo Place,
Leamington Spa CV32 5LA
Tel: 01926 744227

© 2001 Hopscotch Educational Publishing

Written by Collette Drifte
Series design by Blade Communications
Illustrated by Susan Hutchison
Printed by Clintplan, Southam

ISBN 1 902239 64 4

In memory of Kiernan and Spencer Frampton.

About the series

Including Lower-achievers in the Literacy Hour is a series of books aimed at enabling all children, regardless of ability, to access the learning requirements set out in the *National Literacy Strategy Framework for Teaching*. There are six books in the series, one for each of the Primary Years 1–6 (Scottish Primary 2–7). They are designed to be used by teachers or other adults working with lower-achievers in the mainstream classroom.

The books offer a structured approach which provides detailed lesson plans to teach specific skills and goals as outlined in the *National Literacy Strategy Framework for Teaching*. The lesson plans cover work at text, sentence and word levels and target a learning objective from each term's work.

Since lower-achievers often learn at a slower rate than other children, and therefore would have some difficulty in covering the whole year's work within that time, the areas and skills which cause the most problems for these children have been addressed. For example, concepts such as sequencing or predicting are included.

A feature of the series is the provision of several resource and generic sheets for each lesson, which are aimed at considerably reducing teacher preparation time. Permission is granted by the author and publisher to photocopy these sheets for educational purposes within the school or organisation that has purchased this book. The sheets are designed to reinforce the teaching point and offer the child an opportunity to practise the skill being taught. The lesson plans also offer several activities to further consolidate the point. These are designed to be done either with an adult providing close support or with a degree of independence.

The generic sheets can be used with the lesson plans as explained or used by the teacher in a different way according to the needs of the children.

On page 5 is a list of assessment focuses which can be used as an individual assessment record for the children. This page is also photocopiable.

About this book

This book is for teachers of children in Year 4 (Scottish Primary 5). It aims to:

■ enable lower-achievers to be introduced to and enjoy a wide range of stories and poems;

■ focus on concepts that are essential for the wider development of the literacy skills of lower-achievers;

■ encourage lower-achievers to tackle challenging and diverse tasks;

■ enable lower-achievers to access aspects of the *National Literacy Strategy Framework for Teaching*.

The book should be seen, however, as part of a wider strategy by the teacher to address the difficulties of lower-achievers. Such children need a great deal of repetition, practice and consolidation. Therefore, the teacher needs to utilise as many resources as possible to ensure a varied approach which offers these.

The professional audience using this book covers a vast range, from the Newly Qualified Teacher facing their first class, to the 'old hands' who have many years' experience behind them and from the teacher who has never worked with lower-achievers before, to the Classroom Assistant who has worked with such children for a long time. Therefore, any scripting or suggestions regarding the delivery of a teaching point can be easily adapted (or even disregarded!) to suit the individual needs of the professional and/or children in question. The whole essence of teaching lower-achievers is to offer individualism and flexibility.

Chapter content

There are three suggested lesson plans in the 'story' chapters and two in the 'poetry' chapters.

Overall aims

These outline the aims for the lessons set out in each chapter.

Featured book/poems

For stories, this section names the book being used, the author and a brief synopsis of the story.

In the case of a poetry chapter, it lists the poems being used, the poet and the page number where there is a photocopiable version of the poems. This can be enlarged for shared reading in the whole-class session.

A feature of all the lesson plans is that the teaching points can be repeated using other texts or poems of the teacher's choice. This is useful if the chosen text is not favoured by the teacher, or if they need to provide more repetition and consolidation of a teaching point.

Intended learning

This sets out the specific aims for each individual lesson within the chapter.

With the whole class

This outlines a whole-class introduction to the lesson. Because the class is together at this point, the lower-achievers will have the support of their peers and also the opportunity to follow the answers to any questions raised by the other children.

With the lower-achievers

This is the main body of the lesson, since it is designed to be done with the lower-achieving group. The adult-led activities are designed to be done together with an adult closely supporting. The activities are designed to utilise an adult, not necessarily the teacher. The independent activities are designed for the lower-achievers to do without as much close support and supervision. However, the term 'independent' does not imply that the child should be left totally unaided or unsupervised. This is something to be decided at the discretion of the adult/teacher, who will know how much the child is capable of doing without support. A lower-achiever may need help at any point in a lesson and should always have access to an adult to provide that help and support.

The activities suggested may be adjusted to suit the needs of the children. They are intended to offer a variety of ways of tackling the same teaching point and are not necessarily a list to be worked through. To cover all the problems of the children would be impossible, so professional judgement has to be used. For example, occasionally cutting and sticking is required, which may be difficult for the child who has problems with motor control – here the adult can assist; some of the activities require writing, so judgement must be used whether the child needs a scribe.

Plenary session

This offers suggestions for what to do with the whole class at the end of the lesson in order to summarise and explore the learning undertaken in the lesson. This should not just be a 'show and tell' session but rather an opportunity for the children to demonstrate their learning. The lower-achievers should be encouraged to play a part in the session.

Acknowledgements

The following is a list of the books and poems that have been referred to or reproduced in this text:

Books

The Tough Princess, text © 1986 Martin Waddell, illustrations © 1986 Patrick Benson. Included by permission of the publisher, Walker Books Ltd, London; *The Owl Tree*, text © 1997 Jenny Nimmo, illustrations © 1997 Anthony Lewis. Included by permission of the publisher Walker Books Ltd, London; *Jolly Roger*, © 1988 Colin McNaughton. Included by permission of the publisher Walker Books Ltd, London; *The Green Kids*, text © 1992 Sam McBratney, illustrations © 1992 Virginia Chalcraft. Included by permission of the publisher Walker Books Ltd, London; *Play ...If You Dare*, Ruth Symes, (Macdonald Young Books, 1999); *Tommy Niner and the Mystery Spaceship*, Tony Bradman, (Puffin Books, 1995); *Lionheart*, Lynne Markham, (Mammoth, 1998); *How To Write Really Badly*, Anne Fine, (Mammoth, 1996); *Dolphin Boy*, Julie Bertagna, (Mammoth, 1999); *Tiger Roars, Eagle Soars* © 1994 Ruskin Bond. Included by permission of the publisher Walker Books Ltd, London.

Poems

'Ghostly Lessons' from *A Blue Poetry Paintbox*, compiled by John Foster, (Oxford University Press, 1994) © Judith Nicholls 2000, reprinted by permission of the author; 'Who's Afraid?' © 1990 John Foster, from *A Blue Poetry Paintbox*, compiled by John Foster, (Oxford University Press, 1994) included by permission of the author; 'Don't Panic' © 1988 Eric Finney, from *Another Second Poetry Book*, compiled by John Foster, (Oxford University Press, 1988), reprinted by permission of the author; 'I Went Back', Gwen Dunn from *Another Second Poetry Book*, compiled by John Foster, (Oxford University Press, 1988) reprinted by kind permission of the author; 'Grudges' from *Another Second Poetry Book*, compiled by John Foster, (Oxford University Press, 1988) © Judith Nicholls 2000, reprinted by permission of the author; 'Chicken Dinner' by Valerie Bloom, from *Another Second Poetry Book*, compiled by John Foster, (Oxford University Press, 1988) reproduced by permission of Cambridge University Press, © 1992 Valerie Bloom; 'Lion Dance' by Trevor Millum from *Let's Celebrate Festival Poems*, compiled by John Foster, (Oxford University Press, 1989) reprinted by permission of the author; 'Minibeasts', 'A waste of time' and 'A little alliteration' by Mike Jubb, reproduced by kind permission of the author; 'Huff', Wendy Cope from *Another Second Poetry Book*, compiled by John Foster, (Oxford University Press, 1988), reprinted by permission of the author; 'Wellie Weather' by Jacqueline Brown from *Another Second Poetry Book*, compiled by John Foster, (Oxford University Press, 1988), reprinted by permission of the author; 'Cottage' by Eleanor Farjeon, from *A Puffin Quartet of Poets*, 1965 edition; 'Little by Little', Michael Rosen from *A Spider Bought a Bicycle and other poems for young children*, selected by Michael Rosen (Kingfisher Books, 1987); 'I HAVE NEVER BEEN SO HAPPY' and 'MONDAY'S CHILD IS RED AND SPOTTY', from *THERE'S AN AWFUL LOT OF WEIRDOS IN OUR NEIGHBOURHOOD* © 1987 Colin McNaughton, reproduced by permission of the publisher Walker Books Ltd, London.

List of assessment focuses

Assessment focus	Chapter	Date achieved/comments
Can the child understand characterisation, verbs and verb tenses, and syllables in multi-syllabic words?	1	
Can the child recognise the chronology of a narrative, identify powerful verbs and use the 'Look, Say, Cover, Write, Check' strategy?	2	
Can the child identify the setting of a story, recognise the impact on verbs of adverbs with the suffix 'ly' and use a dictionary with the first letter of a word?	3	
Can the child recognise poems on the same theme, identify rhyming couplets and express preferences and opinions about poetry?	4	
Can the child empathise with poems about familiar experiences and identify different styles of poetry?	5	
Can the child recognise stories in series, identify adjectives on a scale of intensity and build words from others with similar patterns and meaning?	6	
Can the child recognise science fiction stories, use the apostrophe for possession in the singular and identify words that imply gender?	7	
Can the child recognise fantasy stories, use the apostrophe for possession in the plural and add suffixes to nouns and verbs to make adjectives?	8	
Can the child appreciate poems from other cultures?	9	
Can the child recognise different patterns of rhyme and verse patterns in poetry?	10	
Can the child identify issues that are raised in stories, recognise how grammar is altered when a sentence type is changed and spell words by analogy to others?	11	
Can the child appreciate stories from other cultures, identify and use appropriately a comma, a colon and a semicolon and use a dictionary with the second letter of a word?	12	
Can the child identify chapters in a book, recognise and use dashes appropriately and use 'it's' and 'its' correctly?	13	
Can the child understand and use the poetical terms 'rhyme', 'rhythm' and 'alliteration' appropriately?	14	
Can the child understand and use the poetical terms 'verse', 'stanza', 'couplet' and 'chorus' appropriately?	15	

Stories and characterisation

Overall aims

- To use the text as a basis for exploring characterisation.
- To revise work on verbs and verb tenses.
- To revise work on syllables and multi-syllabic words.

Featured book

The Tough Princess by Martin Waddell and Patrick Benson (Walker Books, 1986)

Story synopsis

Princess Rosamund is a princess who should have been a prince. She would then have been able to help her parents out of their poverty. But, as a princess, she might be useful anyway – she could marry a rich prince and solve all the family's problems. Unfortunately, Rosamund is not a typical princess. She would much rather be out thumping bad fairies, killing dragons and tossing away uninteresting princes. Rejecting all attempts by her parents to marry her off, she finally finds a husband in her own way and in her own time. She is certainly a princess who turns all previous concepts and ideas of fairytale characters on their heads!

Lesson One

Intended learning

- To use the text as a basis for studying characterisation.
- To be able to use the text to justify views about the main character.
- To explore other texts for characterisation.

With the whole class

- Show the cover of *The Tough Princess* to the children and ask what they think the story might be about. Does the title give them any clues? Do they think it is a fairytale? Why do they think this? Does the title give them an idea about the kind of princess they are going to read about? Ask them to suggest a few words that might describe the princess, for example 'cheeky', 'clever', 'naughty' 'interesting' and 'different'. Write the words on the board and leave them up. The children can revisit them when they have heard the story.

- Share the first part of *The Tough Princess* with the children, letting them see the illustrations. Ask them again what sort of person they think Princess Rosamund is, based on what they have read so far. How do they know? Look at the words on the board and, together, decide if they are accurate. Add any new words the children suggest and leave them up for both the group work and the plenary session.

- Read the rest of the book, encouraging discussion about Princess Rosamund's character. When you have finished, explore some of the following ideas together. Is Rosamund a typical fairytale princess? Why not? What do her escapades tell the reader about her character, for example when she thumps the bad fairy or kills the dragon? Do the children prefer this type of princess to the usual fairytale stereotype? Why or why not?

- Revisit the words written up at the start of the session. Were the children's ideas about Rosamund's character accurate? Invite them to add some new words to the list. Encourage them to justify their words by telling you something from the story that supports them.

- Ask the children how they made a decision about Rosamund's character. What strategies did they use? For example, judging her behaviour in certain situations, deciding whether they liked or disliked what she said, measuring her reactions to other people against what they think they might have done, and so on. Write a few key words and phrases on the board and leave them up. Explain that in all books, stories and plays, this is how we, as readers, form an idea of the characters.

- Encourage the children to suggest other stories with a character they particularly liked or disliked. Ask them to explain why. List the titles on a sheet of paper and leave it for the children to refer to when choosing books.

With the lower-achievers

With adult support

Choose from:

1 Look at a collection of fairytales together and choose two or three favourites. Encourage the children to use the events and incidents in the stories to form views on the main characters. For example, Little Red Riding Hood is kind (for visiting her sick grandma), naive (for believing the wolf to be friendly), gullible (for thinking that the wolf is her grandma) and sensible (for shouting to the woodcutter for help). Help the children to list the characteristics they decide on. Encourage them to write a sentence or two, giving support where necessary.

2 Using Resource sheet 1a, ask the children to tick the Yes/No boxes beside the descriptive words relating to Princess Rosamund. They should then complete the sentence about Princess Rosamund. Give support where necessary.

3 Revisit the words that describe Princess Rosamund written up in the whole-class session. Read these together and help the children to refer to the text for evidence that supports these descriptions.

4 Prepare a set of cards with a 'character word' written on each. You could use the words from the whole-class session together with other adjectives. These might include, for example, 'brave', 'happy', 'silly', 'naughty' and 'boring'. Play two games with the cards. In the first game, each child takes a card, reads the word and then decides whether or not it describes Rosamund. If the others agree, the child keeps the card. The winner is the child with the most cards at the end of the game. In the second game, each child takes a card, reads the word and then tries to suggest a fairytale character who fits the description. Again, if the others agree, the child may keep the card. The winner is the child with the most cards at the end.

Teacher-independent activities

Choose from:

1 Give the children copies of Resource sheet 1a to complete. If necessary read it with them first.

2 Prepare a set of cards with a 'character word' written on each. You could use the words from the whole-class session together with other adjectives. These might include, for example, 'brave', 'happy', 'silly', 'naughty', 'boring' and so on. Ask the children to make a 'Rosamund word wall' using Generic sheet 1 (page 117). They take cards in turn, read them and decide whether or not the word describes Rosamund. If it does, they should write it on a 'brick' in the wall.

3 Select a short section from a fairytale and ask the children to role-play it. Stress that they need to do this quietly. They should decide who is to be individual characters from the story and then in the role-play try to convey the various aspects of the characters, such as bravery, wickedness and so on. Say they will be asked to give a performance at the plenary session.

Plenary session

Before starting the session, cover the words that were written during the whole-class session.

■ Ask the children to tell you the strategies they used to decide about the character in a story. Uncover the key words and check their suggestions against these. Were any strategies left out? Were any new strategies suggested?

■ Look at the list of words describing Rosamund that was written in the whole-class session. Does everybody agree that they are accurate? Has anybody discovered a character in another story who fits some (or all) of the words?

■ Let the children who prepared a role-play show it to the class. Ask the rest of the class to say which characteristics are being portrayed.

Lesson Two

Intended learning

■ To revise work on verbs and verb tenses.

■ To understand and use correctly the terms 'verb', 'past tense', 'present tense' and 'future tense'.

■ To use the featured book as a basis for exploring verbs.

With the whole class

■ Write a few simple verbs on the board such as 'jump', 'want', 'laugh' and 'walk'. Ask the children to tell you what they are. Did they use the term 'verb'? If necessary, remind them of it and challenge them to give you a definition.

■ Together, look through *The Tough Princess* for some verbs. Ask for volunteers to write the verbs on the board. Leave them up while working on this lesson.

■ Remind the children of the work done on verb tenses in previous years. Ask them whether they can remember what the tenses are (past, present and future). Challenge them to tell you the past, present and future tenses of one of the verbs on the board from *The Tough Princess*, using the pronoun 'she'. For example, 'She jumped, she jumps, she will jump'.

■ Play a game of 'Verb and Tense'. One child asks another to give a specific verb tense and the second child has to give the correct response. For example, David says *"Baljinder, the future tense of 'jump',"* and Baljinder replies, *"I will (or I shall) jump."* Then Baljinder says *"Max, the past tense of 'walk',"* and Max replies, *"I walked".* This could become a team game, with the children adding periods of time, such as *"I walked three hours ago"* and *"I jumped two weeks ago".*

With the lower-achievers

With adult support

Choose from:

1 Choose several (according to ability) verbs from *The Tough Princess*. You could use some of those

on the board from the whole-class session. Help the children to decide the past, present and future tenses of each one. They should write these using either 'I' or 'She'. (Make sure that the verb and subject agree.) For example, 'She thumped', 'She thumps' and 'She will thump'.

2 Give the children copies of Resource sheet 1b and ask them to identify the verb tenses. They should write these on the targets.

3 Prepare some cards and divide them into three sets. On one set write some different verbs, on another set write 'past tense', 'present tense' or 'future tense' and on the remaining set write personal pronouns. Place the cards face down in three piles, 'verbs', 'tenses' and 'pronouns'. Tell the children to take a card from each pile and write a sentence with the words on the cards. For example, 'laugh', 'future tense' and 'they' will give 'They will laugh'.

Teacher-independent activities

Choose from:

1 Let the children complete Resource sheet 1b working in pairs. They should discuss each sentence and agree the answer.

2 Prepare a sheet of A4 paper for each pair of children, divided into three columns, headed 'Past tense', 'Present tense' and 'Future tense'. Ask them to write two or three examples of verbs from *The Tough Princess* in each column using 'She'. They could use some of the verbs on the board from the whole-class session.

3 The children could play the same 'past tense', 'present tense', 'future tense' game as described in the adult-led section above.

Plenary session

■ Let some of the children come to the board and write a few verbs. Together, decide sentences for the verbs and write them on the board. Make sure each of the tenses is included.

■ Invite the children to tell you the correct terms for action words ('verbs') that have already happened ('past tense'), are happening now ('present tense') or will happen later ('future tense').

Lesson Three

Intended learning

- To revise work on syllables and multi-syllabic words.
- To use the text as a basis for exploring syllables and multi-syllabic words.
- To use other texts for identifying multi-syllabic words.

With the whole class

- Write 'syllable' on the board and ask the children to read it and tell you what it means. Remind them of the work they did on syllables in previous years. Ask them to give you words with one, two or three syllables. Write them on the board, split into their syllables. For example, write 'computer' as 'com-pu-ter'. Spend a little time revising this with the class, making sure they understand what a syllable actually is.

- Use the children's names to clap and count syllables. Split the class into two. One half claps and chants two or three of the names in that group in turn and the other half counts the number of syllables. Write each name and the number of syllables on the board. For example, Wayne – 1, Sukvinder – 3.

- Challenge the children to give you examples of four- or five-syllable words, for example 'millennium' or 'tyrannosaurus'. (They can often tell you words that they hear in their everyday lives but would be unable to spell or read.) Write them on the board.

With the lower-achievers

With adult support

Choose from:

1   Make sure the children have understood what syllables are. Use musical instruments to 'beat out' the number of syllables in the children's addresses, favourite football teams, pop stars' names and so on. Make a list of these and when you have agreed the number of syllables, let the children write the number next to each name.

2   Give the children copies of Resource sheet 1c to complete. Encourage the use of dictionaries for the last activity.

3   Look at the title page of *The Tough Princess*. Help the children to work out how many syllables there are in each word and then write the words with the number of syllables beside them.

4   Challenge the children to make up a sentence in which all the words have the same number of syllables, for example 'Paul hates this jam' (1) and 'Peter hadn't eaten any apples' (2).

Teacher-independent activities

Choose from:

1   Ask the children to work in pairs to write a simple syllable poem or rhyme. For example a counting poem, where the first line has a one-syllable word, the second has two and so on. For example, 'One bird, Two rabbits, Three elephants,' and so on. They could use an animal encyclopedia to help them.

2   Give the children copies of Resource sheet 1c to complete. Encourage them to use dictionaries for the last activity.

3   Prepare a set of cards with '1 syllable', '2 syllables' or '3 syllables' written on them. Ask the children to work in pairs. Give them a topic, such as 'food' or 'sport'. In turn, they take a card and say a word containing that number of syllables which is related to the topic. They should write the word and the number of syllables. They can use a variety of resources to help them find the words.

Plenary session

- Do all the children understand what a syllable is? Ensure that everybody can identify the correct number of syllables in a given word. Ask each child to tell you how many syllables their name has.

- Allow each group to share what they have done.

- What was the highest number of syllables in one word? What was the word?

Name _____

■ Read the words on the castle. Do you agree that they describe Princess Rosamund? Put a ✔.

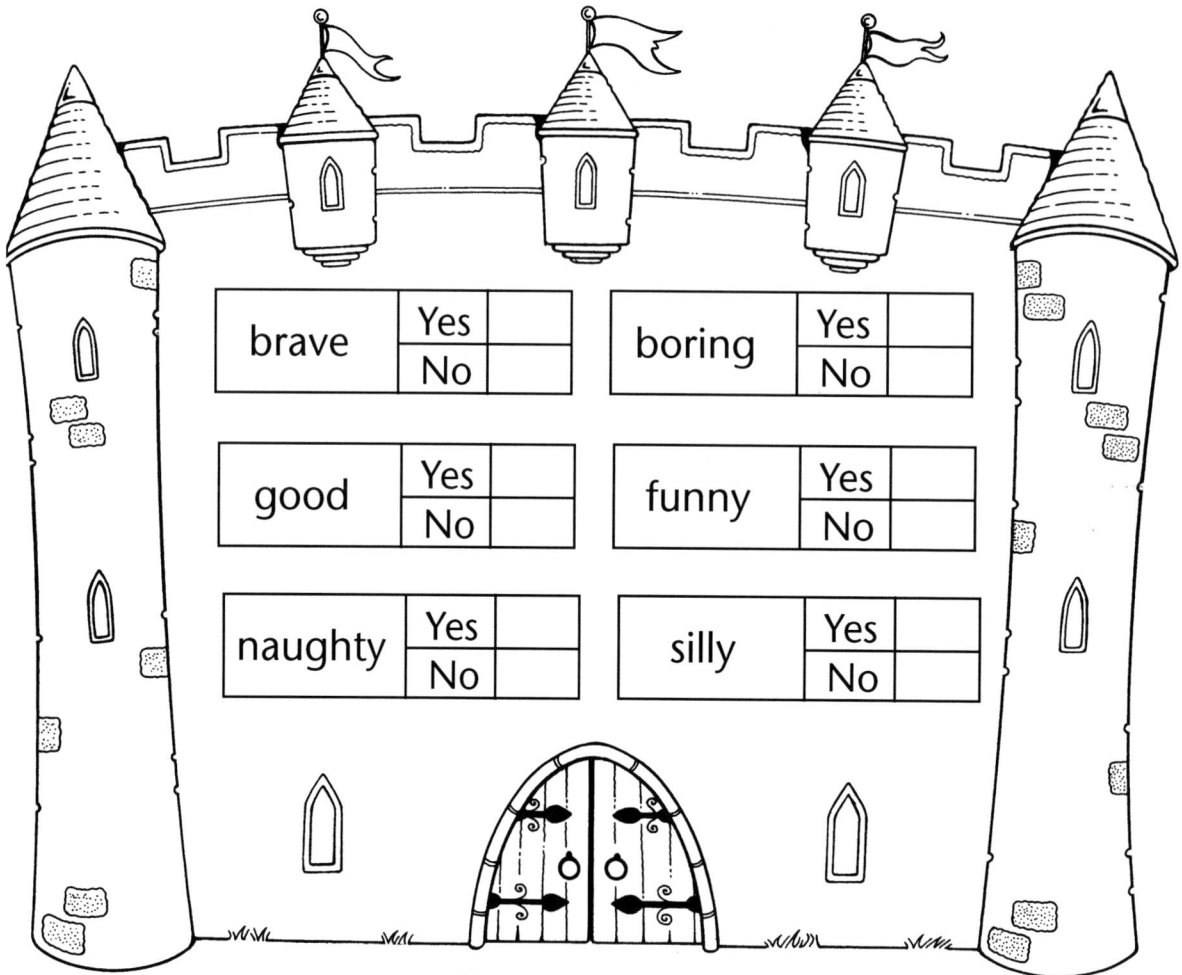

brave	Yes	
	No	

boring	Yes	
	No	

good	Yes	
	No	

funny	Yes	
	No	

naughty	Yes	
	No	

silly	Yes	
	No	

■ Finish the sentence.

I think Princess Rosamund is _____

because _____

_____

_____

Name _____

■ Read the verbs on the arrows. Write past, present or future on the targets.

I am writing. ➡

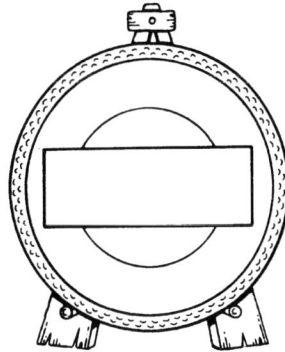

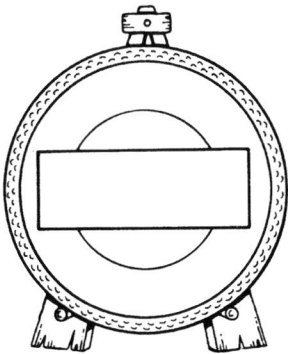

⬅ You jumped. ◄

She will swim. ➡

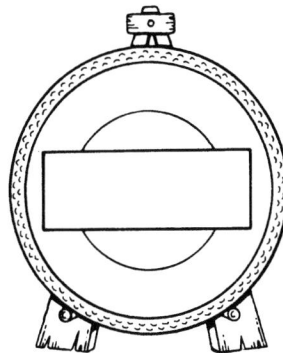

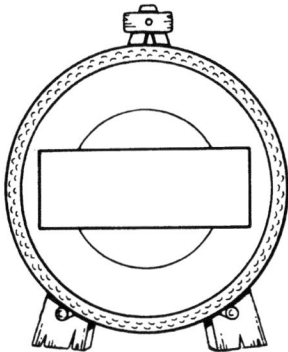

⬅ They will eat. ◄

He walked. ➡

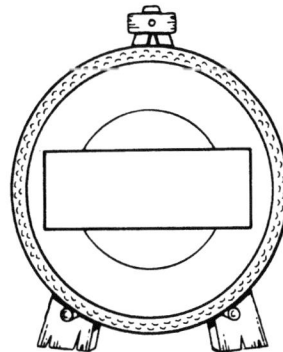

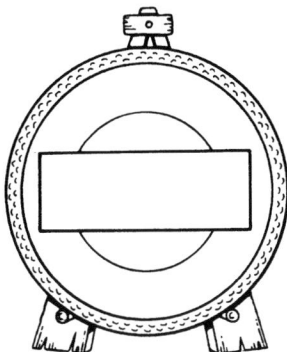

⬅ He is sleeping. ◄

Name _____

■ How many syllables are in each word?

| 1 | 2 | 3 |

frog

□

princess

□

king

□

bicycle

□

dinosaur

□

castle

□

■ Write two words with four syllables.

_____   _____

Stories and chronology

Overall aims

- To explore chronology in narrative.
- To identify the use of powerful verbs, using the text as a basis.
- To practise spellings using the 'Look, Say, Cover, Write, Check' strategy.

Featured book

The Owl-Tree by Jenny Nimmo
(Walker Books, 1997)

Story synopsis

Joe and Minna go to stay with Granny Diamond, whose garden is overhung by a huge, beautiful and mysterious tree – the owl-tree. Mr Rock is threatening to cut down the tree, which means everything to Granny Diamond. She has loved it dearly since she saw a barn owl in it. Joe sees how the life drains out of Granny Diamond as the felling day approaches. He decides that he will overcome his fear of Mr Rock, who has a reputation for being fearsome and hard, to save the tree.

Lesson One

Intended learning

- To explore the chronology of the chosen story.
- To identify words and phrases which illustrate the passage of time.
- To explore how time passes in the narrative of other texts.

With the whole class

- Read the title of the book with the children and ask what they think the story might be about. Discuss the illustration on the cover. Have the children any idea what an 'owl-tree' might be?
- Explain that this story takes place over a period of time and that they should listen carefully and try to notice how the writer makes time pass. Ask them to suggest any words or phrases that they might come across in the narrative to show

this. List some of their suggestions and leave them on the board for reference later.

- Read the first two chapters of *The Owl-Tree* to the children and ask them how they know that time has passed in the story. Discuss together the chronology of the story so far. Some of the following stages could be highlighted: Joe and Minna settle into Granny Diamond's house, Joe sees the 'owl-tree' and Mr Rock, the reasons why Joe and Minna have come to Granny Diamond's are explained, they have tea with Granny who explains about Mr Rock and the tree, the Ludd children are introduced in the 'trick or treat' episode and finally Joe's day ends with him in bed wondering about the mystery of Mr Rock and the tree.

- Look through the first two chapters again in more detail. Invite the children to tell you some of the words and phrases that show the passage of time, for example 'And then', 'in half an hour', 'that night', 'next morning' and 'the day had been … but now'. Write these beside the list drawn up at the beginning of the session and compare the two. Had the children predicted any of the words or phrases?

- Consider a number of fairy tales or other well-known stories. Which take place over a longer period of time? For example, 'Cinderella' or 'Snow White and the Seven Dwarfs' have a longer timespan than 'Goldilocks and the Three Bears'. Explain that however long or short the timespan, every story has its own chronology or sequence of events.

- Continue to read *The Owl-Tree*, pausing where appropriate to highlight the chronology of the narrative. Encourage the children to be aware of this too.

With the lower-achievers

With adult support

Choose from:

1   Write on the board a few phrases, some (but not all) showing the passage of time – for example, 'The next day', 'Later that night', 'The baby smiled', 'Do you like sweets?' Help the children to read these and decide which ones show time passing. Together, discuss how and

why these phrases help to move a story on. Look again at some of the phrases in *The Owl-Tree* and help the children to write them on a chart. Keep this on display and use it for reference when working with other texts.

2 Let the children choose another favourite story or tale. Read this together, asking the children to listen for the types of phrases that were explored in the whole-class session. Ask the children to stop you and tell you the phrase when they hear one. Are these already on the board? Are there some phrases that appear often in different stories?

3 Using Resource sheet 2a, ask the children to draw a circle round the phrases that show the passage of time. Give reading support where necessary. Encourage them to think of some others. They could refer to other storybooks to help them.

Teacher-independent activities

Choose from:

1 Give the children copies of Generic sheet 2 (page 118). In pairs, they should practise telling the story using phrases that show the passage of time between each picture. Say that they should use as many different ones as possible, not always 'and then'. They can tell the stories at the plenary session.

2 Let the children complete Resource sheet 2a. Ask the children to use one or two of the phrases to write some sentences on the back of the sheet.

3 Ask the children to work in pairs to read one or two favourite fairytales (provide texts at a suitable reading level). They should identify which phrases mark the passage of time and either write them down or record them onto a cassette.

Plenary session

■ Did any of the children find words or phrases that were used in several different texts? Ask them to come to the board and write the ones that they came across more than once or twice. Did anybody find a new or very different phrase that showed the passage of time?

■ Look again at the list written during the whole-class session and ask whether anybody found some of these in other texts.

■ Ask the children who prepared the story of 'Jack and the Beanstalk' to tell it to the class. How many different phrases showing the passage of time can the class spot?

Lesson Two

Intended learning

■ To identify the use of powerful verbs, using the text as a basis.

■ To offer alternatives to given verbs.

■ To understand the term 'synonym' and use it correctly.

With the whole class

■ Remind the children of the work they did on verbs before. Invite some of them to write their own examples of verbs on the board.

■ Now give them some other verbs and challenge them to suggest an alternative for each of them, writing it alongside the original in a different colour, for example 'yell' or 'shriek' for 'shout'. Model using a thesaurus to find more words.

■ Explain that these alternatives are called synonyms. Write 'synonym' on the board and read it with the children. Challenge them to give you synonyms for the verbs that were written on the board at the start of the lesson.

■ Tell the children you are going to read the first two chapters of *The Owl-Tree*. They should listen for verbs that make the meaning of the story more powerful or graphic. For example, 'snapped', 'muttered', 'burst (through the gate)' and so on. If necessary, give them some help to start. List the verbs from the chapters and ask the children for synonyms. For example, 'said' for 'snapped', 'answered' for 'muttered' and 'came into the garden' for 'burst through the gate'. Which do the children think are more powerful? Why? Why did the author use 'snapped' rather than 'said'?

With the lower-achievers

With adult support

Choose from:

1   Working closely with the children, look again through some passages from *The Owl-Tree*. Help them to find powerful, expressive verbs. If they need a start, remind them of the verbs that they explored during the whole-class session ('snapped' instead of 'said', 'muttered' instead of 'answered', 'burst through the gate' instead of 'came into the garden'). Help them to list the verbs they find in the passages and encourage them to suggest synonyms. Write the synonym(s) beside each original verb.

2   Work with a copy of Generic sheet 2 (page 118). Together tell the story of 'Jack and the Beastalk' but try to find more interesting verbs. For example, 'Jack's mother was angry' could be improved with words such as 'furious' or 'livid'. Encourage the children to come up with as many different suggestions as possible. They should use a thesaurus to help them. Scribe or record the final version of the story.

3   Give the children copies of Resource sheet 2b. Ask them to read the verbs and draw a circle around the synonyms.

Teacher-independent activities

Choose from:

1   Let the children complete Resource sheet 2b. Ask them to write a sentence on the back of the sheet using one (or more) of the synonyms.

2   Prepare Generic sheet 1 (page 117) by writing a simple verb in each 'brick'. (You could use some of the verbs from the high and medium frequency word lists in the *NLS Framework for Teaching*.) Working in pairs, ask the children to look in a thesaurus for synonyms for each verb and write them in the 'bricks'.

3   Organise the children into pairs. Give each pair a copy of Generic sheet 2 (page 118). They should agree a version of the story using as many interesting verbs as possible. They could record their story onto a cassette.

Plenary session

■   Ask for a volunteer to tell you the correct term for an alternative word ('synonym'). Help them to write it on the board, or write it yourself and help the children to read it.

■   Read or play one of the stories of 'Jack and the Beanstalk' to the class. What interesting verbs do they hear? Write them on the board.

■   Ask a volunteer to explain how and why more powerful verbs help to make a story more interesting.

Lesson Three

Intended learning

■   To use the text to revise and practise the 'Look, Say, Cover, Write, Check' strategy.

■   To use the 'Look, Say, Cover, Write, Check' strategy to learn and consolidate some of the medium frequency words from the *NLS Framework for Teaching*.

With the whole class

■   Write on the board several words from *The Owl-Tree* that the children are unlikely to have learned how to spell, such as 'ghostly', 'silence', 'mention' and 'onions'. Ask who knows how to spell them and then ask a volunteer from the rest of the class to help you to demonstrate the 'Look, Say, Cover, Write, Check' strategy.

■   Ask the children to choose one of the unknown words and then help them to learn how to spell it by using the strategy. Ask other children to help you to demonstrate the strategy using one of the other words. Talk through all the stages for each word learned.

■   Ask for volunteers to model the method on the board without your help. They should talk through the stages in the same way that you did.

With the lower-achievers

With adult support

Choose from:

1   Together, choose three or four words from *The Owl-Tree* to use as 'practice pieces'. (Since it is the technique that is being consolidated, it is acceptable for the children to choose easy words.) Help them to learn the spellings using the 'Look, Say, Cover, Write, Check' strategy. Do this as a group activity, using the board. Challenge the children to learn a few more spellings without your help.

2   Write the following words on Resource sheet 2c, on the lines provided – 'does', 'might', 'used', 'goes', 'told' and 'write'. Make enough copies for the children to have one each. Help them to learn the medium frequency words using this 'Look, Say, Cover, Write, Check' strategy.

3   Use Resource sheet 2c again, this time with the following words from the *NLS Framework for Teaching* – 'walk', 'walked', 'walking', 'brought', 'bought' and 'thought'.

Teacher-independent activities

Choose from:

1   Write the following words on Resource sheet 2c, on the lines provided – 'does', 'might', 'used', 'goes', 'told' and 'write'. Make enough copies for the children to have one each. They could test each other when they have learned the words.

2   Prepare Resource sheet 2c with other words for the children to learn in this way.

3   Let the children work in pairs to practise the strategy freely on the board. Give them a few words from the medium frequency list to learn. Tell them to erase and rewrite as often as they wish.

Plenary session

■   Ask if anybody can tell you how each stage of the strategy works. Ask the other children to listen carefully and see if they agree.

■   Ask for volunteers to spell some of the 'new' words they learned using the strategy.

■   Let the children who completed Resource sheet 2c show the others how the sheets were used.

Name _____

■ Draw a circle round the words that show the passage of time.

Can I eat this?

The next day

and then

Two days later

The dog ran fast

Later that night

Sit down here

After four years

■ Think of some more words that show the passage of time. Write them on the back of this sheet.

■ Read the verbs and circle their synonyms.

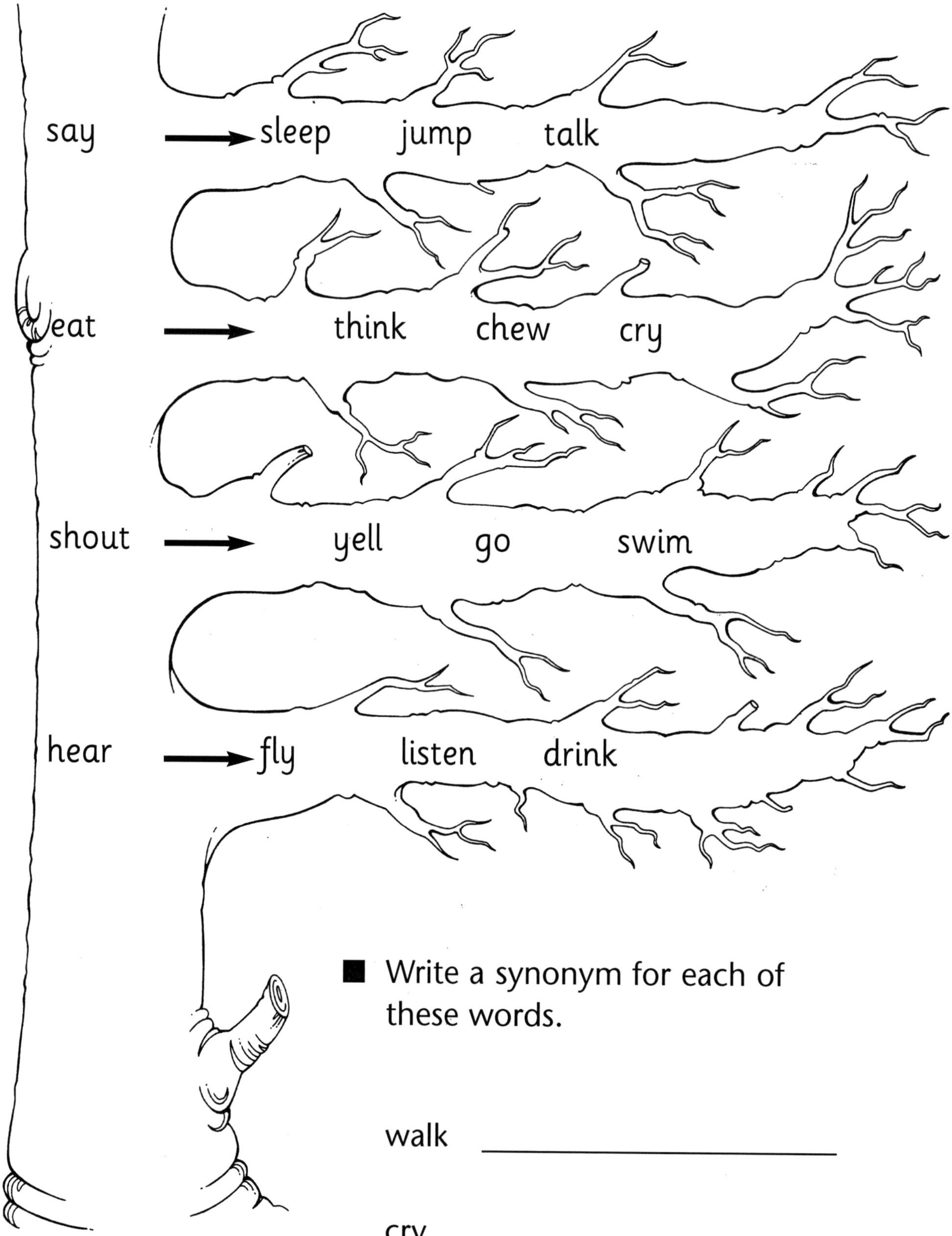

say ➝ sleep   jump   talk

eat ➝   think   chew   cry

shout ➝   yell   go   swim

hear ➝ fly   listen   drink

■ Write a synonym for each of these words.

walk _____

cry _____

■ Follow the numbers.

1 Learn the
words underneath 2.

5 Write

_____

_____

_____

_____

_____

_____

2 Look

_____ _____

_____ _____

_____ _____

6 Check

fold

3 Say

4 Cover

Stories with different settings

Overall aims

- To identify the settings of a range of stories, using information from the text.

- To identify adverbs with the suffix 'ly' and understand how they impact on verbs.

- To use a dictionary referring only to the first letter of a word.

Featured books

Jolly Roger by Colin McNaughton (Walker Books, 1998)

The Green Kids by Sam McBratney (Walker Books, 1993)

Story synopses

These two stories both feature children, but in very different settings. *Jolly Roger* is set aboard a pirate ship, at some unspecified time in the past, but very much tongue-in-cheek and with a good deal of humour. *The Green Kids* is set on a mountain and features children who have very twentieth-century attitudes, which are called into question. Both stories have a happy ending, although they are very different in format, content and style.

Lesson One

Intended learning

- To compare the settings of the featured books and discuss the similarities and differences in the stories.

- To identify the settings of other stories, using information from the text.

With the whole class

- Show the cover of *Jolly Roger* to the children and ask them to guess where and when the story might be set. Write a few key words on the board to refer to later and see how accurate the children were.

- Read *Jolly Roger*, showing the children the text and illustrations. At the end, discuss the setting

again, looking back at the children's predictions. How accurate were they? Explore the language, the illustrations and the story itself as clues for the book's historical setting. Do the children think the story could really have happened? Did they find it a funny book? Why or why not?

- Tell the children that they are going to hear another story about children, but the setting is very different. Show them the cover of *The Green Kids* and ask them to guess where and when the story might be set. Again, write a few key words on the board to refer to later and see how accurate the children were.

- Read *The Green Kids* to the children, allowing them to see the illustrations. Again, ask them when and where the story is set, using clues such as the mention of a television satellite dish, a freezer and a television. Do they think this story would be as effective had it been in a historical setting? Why or why not?

- Divide the board into two sections headed 'Similarities' and 'Differences'. Together, discuss how the two stories are similar and different. For 'Similarities' explore some of the following points: the children are unhappy (for various reasons) at the beginning of both stories but are happy at the end; humour plays an important part in both stories; the parents in both books are self-absorbed at the beginning, but become more aware of others at the end. For 'Differences' explore some of the following points: the settings are different in both time and place; the parents in *The Green Kids* are very wealthy, but Mum in *Jolly Roger* is poor; there is a serious element in *The Green Kids* represented by Mr Collins, who teaches the children about the environment, but there is nothing like this in *Jolly Roger*. Write on each half of the board the main points that come out of the discussion. Leave these up for use in the group activities.

With the lower-achievers

With adult support

Choose from:

1   Ensure that the children understand how the two stories have different settings. Go over the points explored during the whole-class session. Encourage the children to look carefully at the

illustrations for clues. For example, the old-fashioned galleon in *Jolly Roger* and the modern car in *The Green Kids*, or the historical costume in *Jolly Roger* and the modern clothes in *The Green Kids*. Explore the language in both books: the old-fashioned words and phrases in *Jolly Roger* and the modern slang in *The Green Kids*. Help the children to write a few sentences about the settings of both books.

2 Give copies of Resource sheet 3a to the children. Ask them to cross out the wrong words in the statements. They should also think of two books or stories they enjoy and fill in the details about them. Give reading support where necessary.

3 Together, explore several other texts with different settings. Help the children to use the narrative, language, story plot, events and so on as clues to compare the stories.

Teacher-independent activities
Choose from:

1 Give the children copies of Resource sheet 3a to complete. They should work in pairs to support each other with reading.

2 Ask the children to work in pairs to plan two stories with different settings. Give each pair two copies of Generic sheet 3 (page 119). They should make notes about each story on the sheets. Remind them to make sure that the stories are different in all aspects. They could then design covers for the two different stories.

3 Generic sheet 3 (page 119) could be used for the children to record the features of the two stories *Jolly Roger* and *The Green Kids*. They should work in pairs to help each other with the writing.

Plenary session

■ Ask the children who completed Resource sheet 3a to tell the others about the books they chose to describe. Did they enjoy those books?

■ Ask the children who used Generic sheet 3 to tell the class about the stories they made up. They should describe the differences between the stories.

■ Remind the children about the strategies they could use to find the setting of a story. These should include the clues in the narrative, the speech and type of language used by the characters, and the illustrations.

■ As a class, plan two different stories. Write the two plans side by side on the board. Did the children enjoy doing this?

Lesson Two

Intended learning

■ To identify adverbs with the suffix 'ly' and understand how they impact on verbs.

■ To use texts to explore adverbs with the suffix 'ly'.

With the whole class

■ Write on the board a list of adverbs with the suffix 'ly', for example 'softly', 'beautifully', 'loudly' and 'cleverly'. Ask what these have in common. If necessary, point out the 'ly' suffix and highlight it in a different colour.

■ Write 'suffix' on the board and explain what a suffix is. Point out that the suffix 'ly' is added to adjectives to form adverbs. Ask the children to identify the adjectives that were changed to give the examples on the board ('soft', 'beautiful', 'loud' and 'clever').

■ Ask for examples of sentences using some of the adverbs and write them on the board. Challenge the children to identify the position of the adverbs (usually immediately before or after a verb). Ask what the adverb does to the verb. Explain how it gives us more information about how the verb is carried out. For example, 'The girl spoke softly' tells us how the girl spoke.

■ Invite some of the children to come and write some other examples of adverbs with the suffix 'ly' on the board. Leave the work on the board for the group and plenary sessions.

■ Look at *The Green Kids* for adverbs with the 'ly' suffix. For example, 'mysteriously' is on page

25, 'darkly' on page 54 and 'heartily' on page 91. (At this stage you might need to point out that the spellings of some words will need to change to add the 'ly', as in 'heartily', 'messily' and 'happily'.) Tell the children you are going to read the sentences first without the adverbs, then again with them. They should listen carefully and decide how the adverbs change the effect of the verbs. Discuss this together.

With the lower-achievers

With adult support

Choose from:

1 Ensure that the children understand the term 'suffix' and that 'ly' is a suffix that forms an adverb. Look again at the examples of adverbs that were discussed in the whole-class session. As a group use dictionaries to find some more.

2 Make a set of cards, some with an adjective that can be turned into an adverb with the suffix 'ly' and some that do not take this suffix, such as 'red' and 'long'. Play a game where the cards are placed face down on the table. The children take a card, read the adjective and decide whether or not it will make an adverb with 'ly'. If they are correct, they win a counter. If they can also give you a sensible example of any adverb with an appropriate verb, they could win a second counter. The winner is the child with the highest number of counters at the end of the game.

3 Give the children copies of Resource sheet 3b to complete. Give support where necessary.

4 Make some adverb cards for 'slowly', 'softly', 'quickly', 'loudly' and so on. Give each child in the group a different action to perform in different ways, such as eating, sitting, writing or reading. The cards should be placed face down and they turn one over and perform in that manner. They could practise this for the plenary session when the rest of the class has to guess the 'ly' adverb.

Teacher-independent activities

Choose from:

1 Give the children copies of Resource sheet 3b to complete. You may need to read it through with them first.

2 Have prepared some sheets of paper with the following written at the top – 'You can eat', 'You can talk', 'You can run' and 'You can read'. Working in pairs, the children work on one sheet to write adverbs that can be used with the verb. They should use dictionaries and thesauruses to help them.

3 Give pairs of children Generic sheet 2 (page 118). They should look at each picture and decide adverbs that go with the verb in each picture, for example how is the beanstalk growing? How is Jack carrying the hen? They should use dictionaries to help them spell the adverbs and write them beneath the pictures.

Plenary session

■ Ask the children who completed Generic sheet 2 to share with the others what they did. Let them read the words they wrote.

■ Let the children who prepared actions for different verbs demonstrate them to the class. Can the others guess the adverb?

Lesson Three

Intended learning

■ To use a dictionary referring only to the first letter of a word.

■ To use the featured text(s) to practise using dictionaries.

■ To be able to use dictionaries when working with other texts.

With the whole class

■ Ask the children to stand in a line in the alphabetical order of the first letter of their first name. If several children share the same initial letter, challenge them to work out where they should stand. Remind them of the work they did on alphabetical order in previous years.

■ Settle the class down again. Where is alphabetical order always used? List their ideas, which should include dictionaries, thesauruses, encyclopedias and telephone directories. Tell the children that today they are going to work with dictionaries. Show them that at the top of every page in a dictionary there are key words that help them to find their way around the pages.

■ Write on the board a selection of words from *Jolly Roger* and *The Green Kids* beginning with different letters. Choose some words that the children may not know the meanings of. Say that you want them to use a dictionary to find the words and discover their meanings. Ask for volunteers to come up and do this. Encourage them to tell you how they know where to look. Invite them to read the definitions. Show the class how the dictionary is divided into alphabetical order. Leave the words on the board for the group session.

■ Let some of the children choose a word from one of the chosen texts and then look for it in the dictionary. Help them to read the definition if necessary.

■ Choose several different types of text – for example, a history book, a science fiction story and a recipe book. Again, encourage the children to choose a word from these and then look for it in the dictionary. Help them to read the definition if necessary.

With the lower-achievers

With adult support

Choose from:

1 Ensure the children have a dictionary each. Help them to look in the dictionary for the words that are on the board from the whole-class session. Read with them the definition of each word. Challenge them to write the words in alphabetical order.

2 Give the children copies of Resource sheet 3c to complete. Give support where necessary.

3 Have prepared two sets of cards, one set with fairly simple words with different initial letters and the other set containing the definitions of those words as they appear in the dictionary the children will use. Mix the cards up and ask the children to sort them into 'word cards' and 'definition cards'. Place the word cards in a pile face down and the definition cards face up all over the table. The children should take turns to turn over a word card and then find the correct definition card.

Teacher-independent activities

Choose from:

1 Let the children complete Resource sheet 3c.

2 Give the children copies of Generic sheet 1 (page 117). Challenge them to write words in the 'brick wall' starting at the top left in alphabetical order. They should use dictionaries to help them.

3 The children should each choose a favourite book and look through it for words they don't know or understand. They should write these down, find them in a dictionary and write the definitions alongside them.

Plenary session

■ Ask a volunteer to tell you how a dictionary is ordered. Make sure they use the term 'alphabetical order'. How do you use a dictionary?

■ Let the children who worked independently with a favourite book tell the class about the words they found. Help them to read the definitions out loud. Make sure everyone understands.

■ Did anyone have a problem finding a word in the dictionary? Did the words at the top of the pages help or not?

■ Make sure the children are all seated near you and ask them to give you words to find in the dictionary. Show them how you look for the word. Do they do the same?

Name _____

■ Cross out the wrong words in these sentences.

'The Green Kids' is set in the past/present/future.
It is set on a ship/mountain/beach.
It is about children/animals/pirates.

'Jolly Roger' is set in the   past   present   future.
It is set on a   beach   planet   ship.
It is about   dragons   pirates   monsters.

■ Choose two storybooks of your own and complete the following charts.

My first storybook is called _____
_____
The time it is set is in the _____
The place it is set is _____
It is about _____

My second storybook is called _____
_____
The time it is set is in the _____
The place it is set is _____
It is about _____

■ Make these adjectives into adverbs by adding the suffix 'ly'.

 loud

 soft

 slow

_____   _____   _____

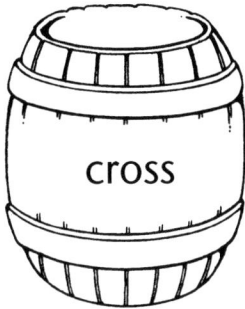 cross

 quiet

 quick

_____   _____   _____

■ Choose one of the adverbs above to finish each sentence.

'Sit down!' the teacher said cr_____

The snail went _____ along the path.

The girls ran away very _____

■ Make up sentences for the other adverbs. Write them on the back of this sheet.

■ Put these words into alphabetical order. You can use the alphabet below to help you. The first one is done for you.

wings	mountain	doll
harbour	~~cottage~~	pirate
ship	trolley	fly

1 <u>cottage</u>   2 _____   3 _____

4 _____   5 _____   6 _____

7 _____   8 _____   9 _____

a b c d e f g h i j k l m n o p q r s t u v w x y z

■ Choose three of the words and look for them in a dictionary. Write what they mean.

_____

_____

_____

Poems with themes

Overall aims

- To explore poems on a similar theme.
- To identify rhyming couplets.
- To be able to form preferences and give reasons for choices.
- To use the chosen poems as a basis for writing own poetry.

Featured books

A Blue Poetry Paintbox compiled by John Foster (Oxford University Press, 1994)

Another Second Poetry Book compiled by John Foster (Oxford University Press, 1988)

Lesson One

Chosen poems

'Ghostly Lessons' by Judith Nicholls, page 30

'Who's Afraid?' by John Foster, page 30

Intended learning

- To read and compare two poems on the theme of ghosts.
- To decide which poem is the favourite and to give reasons for the choice.
- To identify rhyming couplets

With the whole class

- Enlarge copies of 'Ghostly Lessons' and 'Who's Afraid?' Tell the children that in the next couple of lessons, they are going to talk about some poems with the same theme – ghosts and monsters.
- Read 'Ghostly Lessons' with the children, letting them follow the text. Ask them what the poem is about. Did they expect a ghost poem to be written from the ghost's point of view? Did they enjoy the poem? Why or why not?
- Tell them they are going to hear another poem like this. Ask them to listen carefully and decide who is 'speaking' in the poem. Read 'Who's

Afraid?', letting the children follow the text. How is this poem similar to the first one? (Again, it is written from the ghost's viewpoint.) Do they understand the double meaning of the title? Who is afraid, those who see the ghost or the ghost doing the haunting?

- Ask several children to tell you which of the two poems is their favourite and why. Tell the children which is your favourite poem and why.
- Tell the children they are going to look for the rhyming words in 'Ghostly Lessons'. Do they remember what rhyming means? If necessary, remind them, giving a few examples as illustration. Ask them to tell you the rhyming words in the poem: 'treat'/'eat', 'heel'/'feel', 'stared'/'scared'. Read the poem again, pausing at the ends of the lines and letting the children supply the rhyming words for each verse.
- Do the same with 'Who's Afraid?': 'tonight'/ 'fright', 'house'/'mouse', 'out'/'about', 'here'/ 'fear'. Ask the children to comment on the position of these rhyming words compared with those of 'Ghostly Lessons'. Point out that they are consecutive rhymes, whereas those in 'Ghostly Lessons' are alternate. Explain that these pairs of consecutive rhyming words are called 'rhyming couplets'.
- Read the poem again with the children, encouraging them to supply the rhyming couplets for each verse.

With the lower-achievers

With adult support

Choose from:

1   Look again at 'Ghostly Lessons' and 'Who's Afraid?' and explore the rhymes in both poems. Focus on the couplets in 'Who's Afraid?' and make sure the children understand that the rhymes are consecutive. Reinforce this by looking at the couplets in some nursery rhymes, such as 'Baa baa black sheep' or 'Little Miss Muffet'. Help the children to write the couplets.

2   Give the children copies of Resource sheet 4a. Help them to join each set of rhyming couplets. Give reading support where necessary.

3   Decide which poem is the group's favourite and discuss why. Allocate a line of the favourite poem to each child and practise learning these until they can put them together and recite the whole poem.

4   Give the children copies of Resource sheet 4b and help them to write the name of their favourite poem and why they like it best. They may use the words on the sheet or their own if they prefer. Give support where necessary.

Teacher-independent activities
Choose from:

1   Make copies of several rhymes or poems. Ask the children to work in pairs and first identify the rhymes by underlining them. They should then decide which have rhyming couplets. Remind the children that couplets comprise consecutive rhymes.

2   Let the children complete Resource sheet 4a and/or Resource sheet 4b.

3   Prepare a set of cards with the rhyming words from a nursery rhyme couplet written on each, for example 'wool' and 'full' on one card, 'dock' and 'clock' on another, and so on. Place the cards on the table face down. The children take one, read the words and say the full couplet from the nursery rhyme. If the others agree they are correct, they keep the card. If not, they replace the card at the bottom of the pile. The winner is the child who has the most cards at the end of the game.

Plenary session

■   Ask a volunteer to tell you what a rhyming couplet is. Make sure they say that the rhymes are consecutive (not alternate). Ask for volunteers to give you examples.

■   Let the children who learned one of the chosen poems recite it for the others.

■   Does anybody like 'Ghostly Lessons' best? Invite them to say why. Does somebody else prefer 'Who's Afraid?' Encourage them to give reasons for their preference.

Lesson Two

Chosen poem
'Don't Panic' by Eric Finney, page 31

Intended learning
■   To continue working with poetry on the theme of ghosts and monsters.

■   To identify the rhyming couplets in the chosen poem.

■   To use the chosen poem as a basis for writing own poetry.

With the whole class
■   Remind the children of the work they did on the ghost poems in Lesson One. Who remembers which poem had rhyming couplets? ('Who's Afraid?') Challenge the children to tell you some of the rhyming couplets. Ask what a rhyming couplet is. Make sure they say that the rhyming words in a couplet are on consecutive lines.

■   Enlarge a copy of 'Don't Panic'. Read it to the children, letting them follow the text. How is this poem different from those they looked at in the previous session? Some of the following ideas can be discussed: this poem is written from the point of view of the person being scared, not the 'scarer's'; the speaker is a human, not a ghost; the subject matter is mainly about monsters rather than ghosts; the monsters are in the speaker's imagination.

■   Ask the children to identify the rhyming couplets in the poem ('pane'/'rain', 'mass'/'glass', 'floor'/'before', 'draught'/'daft', 'makes'/'snakes', 'riders'/'spiders', 'gloom'/'room'). You could talk about how the sounds of words vary with accents, so to some people 'mass'/'glass' and 'draught'/'daft' might not rhyme. 'Mean' and 'in' certainly don't rhyme! But with poetry we can play with the language and the sounds. This makes poetry fun.

■   Discuss with the children what things they are afraid of in the dark. List them. Together, compose a class poem using 'Don't Panic' as a model. Say that the poem doesn't have to rhyme although if together they can make rhyming couplets that would be fun. Display the poem while working on this lesson.

With the lower-achievers

With adult support

Choose from:

1 Look again at 'Don't Panic' and ask the children to identify the rhyming couplets. Use Generic sheet 1 (page 117) to write on the 'bricks' in the word wall each rhyming pair from the couplets.

2 Give the children copies of Resource sheet 4c and help them to write a poem about either ghosts or monsters. To get them started, revisit the class poem written during the whole-class session. Remind them that their poem does not have to rhyme. They can use either their own words or the words on the sheet.

3 Prepare a set of cards with one rhyming word from a nursery rhyme couplet written on each, for example 'corner', 'fiddle', 'wool' and so on. Record on a cassette the other half of each couplet ('Horner', 'diddle', 'full' and so on), leaving a few seconds between each word to allow for stops. (Alternatively, make cards for these words.) Place the cards on the table face up. The children listen in turn to the cassette and find the card that matches the recorded word. If they are correct, they keep the card; if not, they replace the card on the table. The winner has the most cards at the end of the game.

Teacher-independent activities

Choose from:

1 Prepare Generic sheet 4 (page 120) with a simple word written on one of each pair of shoes. You could take the words from the medium frequency list for Years 4 and 5 in the *NLS Framework for Teaching*. The children should write a rhyming word in the other half of each pair. For example, you could supply 'show' and the child might write 'know' or 'blow'. Ask them to use the rhyming words to make a rhyming couplet.

2 Let the children complete Resource sheet 4c in pairs. Read it through with them first and tell them to try to make their poem rhyme if they can.

3 Before the session, enlarge copies of 'Who's Afraid?' and 'Don't Panic', stick them on card and cut each one up into its separate lines. (Put each set of lines into different envelopes to avoid the two poems becoming mixed up.) The children should spread the lines out on the table and then put the rhyming couplets together. They can check against the enlarged copy from Lesson One whether they were right.

Plenary session

■ Make sure everybody understands what a rhyming couplet is.

■ Ask the children who wrote their own poems to read them to the rest of the class.

■ Which poem of all three explored is the children's favourite? Let them tell you why.

Ghostly Lessons

Mum, I want some chocolate,
just one little treat –
peppermint or strawberry cream…
GHOSTS DON'T EAT!

Mum, I've got a toothache,
a pain in my heel;
my throat's too sore to work tonight…
GHOSTS DON'T FEEL!

Mum, I really hate the dark –
I hate the way they stared!
I'm scared of graveyards, woods and folk…
GHOSTS AREN'T SCARED!

Judith Nicholls

Who's Afraid?

Do I have to go haunting tonight?
The children might give me a fright.
It's dark in that house.
I might meet a mouse.
Do I have to go haunting tonight?

I don't like the way they scream out,
When they see me drifting about.
I'd much rather stay here,
Where there's nothing to fear.
Do I have to go haunting tonight?

John Foster

Don't Panic

That beating at my bedroom pane:
It's only wind and driving rain.
Relax.

That awful blind and blurry mass:
Nothing but rain streaks on the glass.
Harmless.

That monstrous shadow leaning in,
Wearing an evil twisted grin:
It's just the ivy plant that's all
Bobbing and tossing on the wall.
Don't panic.

That scratching from my bedroom floor:
It's just a mouse, he's been before.
No sweat.

That rustling – is it just the draught?
Or giant spiders? Don't be daft!
Couldn't be.

The loops this new wallpaper makes:
Just loops, not coiled and deadly snakes.
Absurd!

Suppose there are though – snakes, I mean,
And evil spirits sidling in,
And ghosts and blobs and phantom riders
And armies of advancing spiders,
And vampires stalking through the gloom,
All closing in upon my room…
HELP!

Eric Finney

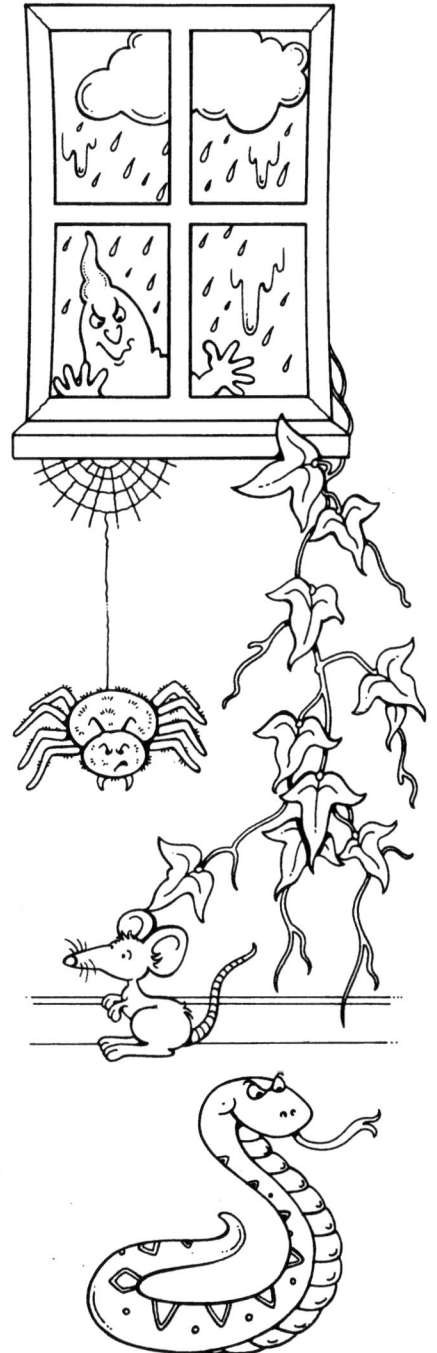

Name _____

■ Join two lines to make a rhyming couplet.
One has been done for you.

In the dark if you get a fright	To meet a monster big and hairy.
A nightmare is a horrible dream	Who sat and ate some beans on toast.
Ghosts can bang and thud and thump	Get out of bed and switch on the light.
Once there was a hungry ghost	In case you see a ghost in the park.
Make sure you're home before the dark	Scary noises that make you jump.
Late at night it's very scary	That's sure to make you want to scream.

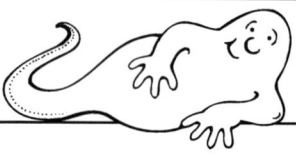

■ Finish the sentences. There are some words to help you at the bottom of the page.

My favourite poem is _____

_____ I like it because

_____

_____

_____

_____

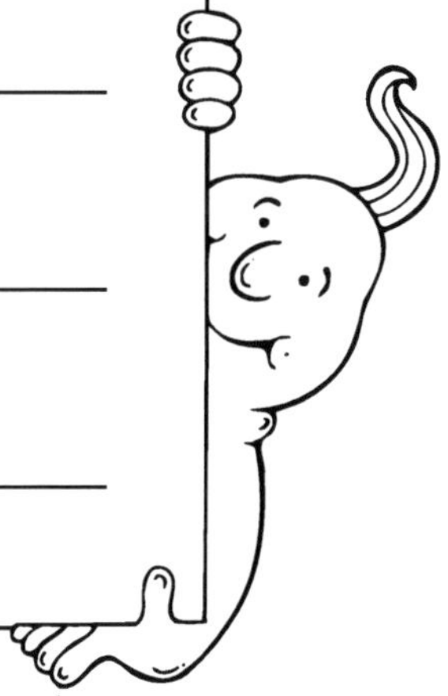

'Ghostly Lessons'   'Who's Afraid?'

scary   funny   don't

ghosts   laugh   usually

different   silly   doesn't

■ Write a poem about ghosts or monsters. Make it rhyme if you can. You can use the words at the bottom of the sheet to help you.

Late at night _____

The sound of _____

In the _____

Suddenly _____

There was _____

And then _____

dark	frightened	monster
ghost	shrieks	howling
nightmare	swoop	terrifying

Poems for writing poetry

Overall aims

- To explore poetry with familiar experiences.
- To compare the styles of different poetry.
- To use the poetry as a basis for own work.

Featured book

Another Second Poetry Book compiled by John Foster (Oxford University Press, 1988)

Lesson One

Chosen poem

'I Went Back' by Gwen Dunn, page 38

Intended learning

- To explore the chosen poem and relate it to own or familiar experiences.
- To use the poetry as a basis for own work.

With the whole class

- Enlarge a copy of 'I Went Back'. Tell the children that in the next couple of lessons, they are going to explore some poems about experiences they may have had themselves.

- Ask the children to read the title of the poem. Before reading the poem, ask for ideas of what it might be about judging from the title. List the children's suggestions on the board.

- Read 'I Went Back', letting the children follow the text. Were they right in their guess at what the poem is about? Did they understand the feelings of the child in the poem? What was it that the child in the poem found unsettling about going back to school? Point out that in the beginning of the poem everything seems to be wrong and the child feels left behind. By the end of the poem, things are getting better and the child feels more in tune with the class. Read the lines that illustrate this – from 'Tuesday's news day...'

- Have the children ever experienced this? Encourage them to describe their own experiences of coming back to school after illness. How did they feel? What did they find strange? Was there anything they were glad had not changed? Were they happy or not to be back? Why did they feel like this?

- Write some of the children's ideas on the board in sentences. Encourage them to describe how they felt.

With the lower-achievers

With adult support

Choose from:

1   Look at the enlarged copy of 'I Went Back' together with the children and read it, encouraging them to follow the text. Ask them to tell you whether the mood of the child in the poem changes. How? Is there a particular line or idea in the poem that the children themselves have experienced, for example feeling upset that they missed the blooming of the daffodils that they planted? Help them to write a sentence or two about this.

2   Give the children copies of Resource sheet 5a. Help them to write about their own feelings on returning to school after an absence.

3   Explore other familiar experiences that would be interesting to write about. Some ideas are going to the doctor, a new baby or a very special surprise birthday present. Choose one of the subjects and together brainstorm ideas for sentences. Help the children to write these. Write a group paragraph that can be shared in the plenary session.

Teacher-independent activities

Choose from:

1   Give the children copies of Resource sheet 5a to complete in pairs.

2   Give pairs of children a copy of 'I Went Back'. Ask them to practise reading the poem aloud, taking a line in turn. If they can do this confidently, they could record it onto a cassette.

3   Give the children copies of 'I Went Back' with some of the nouns whited out. For example, 'They'd made a _____', 'Learnt a song about _____' and 'Jean had a new _____.'

Ask the children to complete the poem with words of their own. This will give them the sense of achievement of having written a poem but the support of a scaffold to work with.

Plenary session

- Share the work the children have done during this session. What have they enjoyed about it?

- Do the children like poems and stories about familiar experiences? Why? Encourage them to give reasons for their answers.

Lesson Two

Chosen poem

'Grudges' by Judith Nicholls, page 39

Intended learning

- To explore the chosen poem and relate it to own or familiar experiences.

- To compare the different styles of the chosen poetry.

- To use the poetry as a basis for own work.

With the whole class

- Enlarge a copy of 'Grudges'. Tell the children that they are going to explore a poem about an experience they may have had themselves. Ask the children what a grudge is. Invite them to guess what the poem is about.

- Read 'Grudges' to the children, letting them follow the text. Do they understand the feelings of the child in the poem? Have they experienced these feelings themselves? What does the child in the poem find annoying about her sister? How do we know that the writer is a girl? ('...her old coats are all I've ever had') Encourage the children to share their own experiences of sibling jealousy or rivalry. How did they feel? What things about their sibling(s) irritate them?

- Read 'I Went Back' again with the children. Ask them how the poems are similar and how they are different. Discuss some of the following ideas: both poems deal with familiar experiences, both are written in the first person singular, both have a rhyming pattern, they have different end-moods ('I Went Back' finishes positively but 'Grudges' ends with the speaker still irritated), the rhyme and rhythm patterns are different ('I Went Back' has irregular patterns but 'Grudges' has regular patterns).

- Encourage the children to suggest other family-based experiences that might be good subjects for a poem. Write them on the board. Some ideas are 'The Morning Rush', 'My New Baby', 'Sharing the Computer' and 'Pocket Money'. Together, decide on a subject and compose a class poem using 'Grudges' as a model. Remind the children that the poem does not have to rhyme. Display it while working on this lesson.

With the lower-achievers

With adult support

Choose from:

1   Divide a large board or sheet of paper into three sections. Give the sections the following headings: 'It isn't fair when ...', 'It isn't right when...' and 'It makes me mad when...' These are lines taken from the poem 'Grudges'. Share ideas for what the children could write under each heading. You could list ideas for each column or write sentences.

2   Give copies of Resource sheet 5b to the children. Help them to write a poem about their brother or sister (children without siblings could write about a sibling they would – or wouldn't! – like to have). They can choose their own words or use the words at the bottom of the sheet.

3   Discuss again the similarities and differences between the two poems. Give the children copies of Resource sheet 5c and help them to match the statements to the books. Give reading support where necessary.

Teacher-independent activities

Choose from:

1   Give the children copies of Resource sheet 5b to complete. You might need to read it through with them first.

2   Ask the children to look through anthologies for poems about family relationships. Ask them to choose one or two to share in the plenary session.

3   Give the children copies of Resource sheet 5c to complete. They should work in pairs to help with the reading. You might need to read it through with them first.

Plenary session

■   Ask the children who found other poems about family relationships to tell the class which their favourite is and why. Invite them to read the poems to the other children or read them yourself if they don't feel confident enough. Do the others like the poems? Why or why not?

■   Ask the children whether they can remember the similarities and the differences between the two chosen poems. Have they enjoyed exploring these poems? Encourage the children to give reasons for their answers.

I Went Back

I went back after a cold
And nothing was the same.
When the register was called
Even my name
Sounded queer … new …
(And I was born here too!)
Everyone knew more than me,
Even Kenneth Hannaky
Who's the worst usually.
They'd made a play
And puppets from clay
While I was away,
Learnt a song about Cape Horn,
Five guinea pigs were born.
Daffodils in the blue pot,
(I planted them)
Bloomed, and I was not
There to see.
Jean had a new coat
And someone, probably
    George,
Smashed my paper boat.
Monday was a dreadful day.
I wished I was still away.
Tuesday's news day.

I took my stamps to show,
Made a clown called Jo,
Learnt that song from John …
Cold's almost gone …
And … the smallest guinea pig,
Silky black and brown thing,
I'm having
Till spring.

Gwen Dunn

Grudges

It isn't fair …
that I must be in bed
for hours before,
that I get all the blame
and never her,
that she's allowed to choose
what she will wear,
it isn't fair!

It isn't right …
that she's allowed out
late at night,
that she can choose when to
switch off her light,
that I'm the one told off
whenever there's a fight,
it isn't right!

It makes me mad …
that they think she's so good
and I'm so bad,
that she gets extra cash
for helping dad,
that her old coats are all
I've ever had,
It makes me mad!

(I know I'm nine
and she is seventeen;
that's no excuse at all
for them to be so MEAN!)

Judith Nicholls

■ Write some sentences about how you felt when you went back to school after being away. There are some words at the bottom of the sheet to help you.

_____

_____

_____

_____

_____

_____

❖ ❖ ❖ ❖ ❖ ❖ ❖ ❖ ❖

happy	strange	bored	sad
friends	tired	lonely	teacher
unsure	glad	frightened	alone

■ Draw a picture and write a poem about your sister or brother. There are some words at the bottom of the sheet to help you.

My _____

My _____ is _____

I _____

_____ always _____

Even if _____

But _____

I _____

❖ ❖ ❖ ❖ ❖ ❖ ❖ ❖ ❖

funny	annoying	fight	play
bossy	share	laugh	fair
naughty	clever	kind	nasty
baby	love	younger	older

■ Draw a line from each sentence to the poem it matches.
Some sentences will match both poems. One has been
done for you.

The poem is
about families.

The poem
ends happily.

Grudges
by Judith Nicholls

I like this
poem.

The poem is
about a child.

I Went Back
by Gwen Dunn

The poem is
about school.

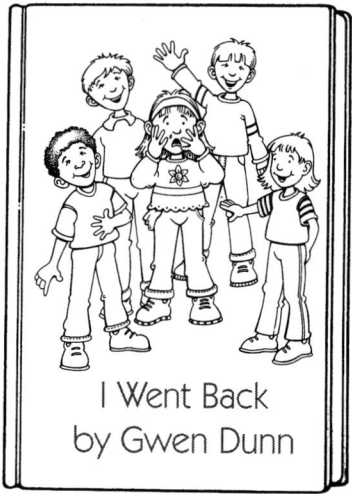

The poem has
verses.

The poem uses
words that rhyme.

Stories in series

Overall aims

- To use the featured book as a basis for introducing one particular series.

- To be able to review a range of other stories in a series.

- To compare adjectives on a scale of intensity.

- To build words from others with similar patterns and meanings.

Featured book

Play … If You Dare by Ruth Symes from the TREMORS series (Macdonald Young Books, 1999)

Story synopsis

Josie buys an amazingly cheap computer game at a car boot sale. The game challenges her to 'Play … if you dare', so she does. As she plays, each level of the game becomes more terrifying until, eventually, it threatens to trap her inside it forever. By skilful playing, Josie manages to escape and helps a trapped boy to do so too, but only after some hair-raising incidents.

The book is one in a series of spine-chilling stories that are written to scare the readers while making them powerless to put the book down!

Lesson One

Intended learning

- To use the featured book as a basis for introducing one particular series.

- To be able to review a range of other stories in a series.

With the whole class

This lesson may take several sessions.

- Tell the children they are going to read a story that is one of a series. Write 'series' on the board and ask them what it means. Where else might they come across this word? For example, a television series or a series of computer games. Discuss what makes a series. You could talk about some of the following ideas: there is always a common thread running through a series, such as the same character or the same subject matter; each part of a series is usually in the same style or format as the others; there is usually a fixed number of parts in a series; the parts of a series often follow on from each other, but they can also be independent.

- Point out the word TREMORS on the front cover of *Play … If You Dare*. Ask for a volunteer to read it and tell you what it means. Tell the children that this book is one of a series called TREMORS. Discuss the illustration on the cover. How do the children feel when they look at the picture? What does the expression on the girl's face convey? Why doesn't the picture have soft lines and gentle colours? Encourage the children to suggest what the TREMORS series might be about, judging from the cover, the title of this book and the series title. Write some key words from their answers on a large sheet of paper and keep it pinned up for reference during the lesson.

- Read *Play … If You Dare*. At the end, ask the children whether they liked the book and why. Were they frightened? Did they think the story would end badly? Would they now like to read more stories from the TREMORS series? Encourage the children to give reasons for their answers.

- Read some (or all!) of the other books in the series: *The Ghosts of Golfhawk Hall* by Tessa Potter, *The Claygate Hound* by Jan Dean, *The Curse of the Ghost Horse* by Anthony Masters.

- Discuss how the books in the series are similar. Explore some of the following ideas: Do the books follow the same format – for example, do they all have chapters, the same kind of punctuation, the same kind of font and so on? Are they all about the same thing, such as ghosts, monsters or frightening situations? Are the books set out in the same way? Are the illustrations similar? Are there pictures in every book? Do all the books have a happy ending? Look again at the key words written at the beginning of the session about the TREMORS series. How accurate were the children's suggestions about the series' content?

■ Explain that other series will have very different themes: horses, books with the same main character, football, school stories and so on. Over the next few weeks, read some series with a variety of subject matter. Encourage the children to discuss their opinions about each series and to decide what common characteristics each series has.

With the lower-achievers

With adult support

Choose from:

1 Give the children copies of Resource sheet 6a. They should read the statements about the TREMORS series and tick the ones with which they agree. Give reading support where necessary. Share the answers and discuss the last two asking them to give their reasons.

2 Continue to discuss with the children the common elements of the books in the TREMORS series. Help them to use the key words written during the whole-class session to focus on the features of the series. Ask them to complete Generic sheet 5 (page 121).

3 Together, choose a book from a different series. Encourage the children to choose a series with a completely different subject matter from TREMORS. Look at the cover of the book. Do the illustration and colours used give an impression of what the book might be like? Read the book together. Is it different from the TREMORS series? In what way? Does the cover accurately represent the story? Would they like to read another book from this series?

Teacher-independent activities

Choose from:

1 Let the children complete Resource sheet 6a in pairs. You may need to read it through with them first.

2 Ask the children to write a few sentences about *Play … If You Dare*, including whether they liked the book and whether they would read more books from the series.

3 Ask the children to work in pairs to devise a new series of books. What would be the theme

running through the books? Who would the characters be? What about the setting and time period? They could use Generic sheet 3 (page 119) to record on, replacing the word 'story' with 'series'. They could then design a cover for one of the books in their series.

Plenary session

■ Encourage the children to tell you what they have learned about books in a series generally, and any series in particular.

■ Do they like stories in a series? Why or why not? Do they think the first book they read in a series would influence their decision to read more? Encourage the children to give reasons for their answers.

■ Ask which series are their favourites and why.

Lesson Two

Intended learning

■ To compare adjectives on a scale of intensity.

■ To use the featured book as a basis for identifying such adjectives.

■ To be able to identify such adjectives in other texts.

With the whole class

■ Remind the children of the work they did in Years 2 and 3 on adjectives. Do any of the children remember what adjectives are? Ask for volunteers to come to the board and write examples of adjectives. Leave these up.

■ Now write on the board 'hot', 'lukewarm', 'warm', 'cold' and 'chilly'. Read them together and then ask the children what they notice about these adjectives. They describe something at different levels of intensity. Ask for a volunteer to put them in order of intensity ('hot', 'warm', 'lukewarm', 'chilly' and 'cold').

■ Write on the board some examples of adjectives from *Play … If You Dare* and ask the children to suggest other adjectives on a scale of intensity.

For example, for 'good' (page 9) the children could offer 'bad', 'poor', 'very good', 'excellent' and 'fantastic'; for 'massive' (page 40) they could suggest 'huge', 'large', 'big', 'medium', 'small', 'tiny' and 'minute'.

■ Look again at the adjectives written on the board by children at the beginning of the session. Invite them to add others of different intensity to these. Let them write the new words on the board next to the originals.

With the lower-achievers

With adult support

Choose from:

1 Give the children some starter adjectives, such as 'fast' and 'big' and ask them to think of other adjectives related to them. They could use dictionaries and thesauruses to help them. They could write these out in order of level of intensity inside an outline drawing, for example in an outline of a thermometer or an outline of a person.

2 Give the children copies of Resource sheet 6b and ask them to put the adjectives in order of intensity. (The order can be from least to most or vice versa as long as it is correct.) Give reading support if necessary.

3 Use Generic sheet 1 (page 117) to help the children to make an 'adjective wall' in which each row of 'bricks' has adjectives at different levels of intensity. You could put starter words from well-known stories in the first 'brick' of each row to get the children going.

4 Stick Resource sheet 6b onto card and cut out the boxes. Using one adjective set at a time, give three children one card each and ask them to come out and stand beside each other in order.

Teacher-independent activities

Choose from:

1 Give the children copies of Resource sheet 6b to complete.

2 Make a set of cards by sticking Resource sheet 6b onto card and cutting out the words. The children could play a game where the cards are shuffled and dealt to the group. Child A puts a

card on the table. If Child B has a related card, they can put it next to the first card; if not, they have to pass the turn to the next child. Only when the three cards from each set have been placed can a fresh set be started. The winner is the first child to place all their cards.

3 Let the children work in pairs. Each pair should choose a different book and read through it looking for adjectives. When they have found one or two they should discuss and agree other related adjectives and write them out in the scale of intensity. They will need dictionaries and thesauruses.

Plenary session

■ Let the children who made sets of related adjectives read these to the others.

■ Ask the children who made an 'adjective wall' to show it to the class and explain how it was made.

■ Does everybody understand how adjectives can be used to express different levels of intensity?

Lesson Three

Intended learning

■ To identify words which have similar patterns or meanings. For example, 'medical' and 'medicine'.

■ To build words from others with similar patterns and meanings.

With the whole class

■ Write on the board 'medicine', 'medical', 'medication'. Ask for volunteers to read the words. What do the words mean? What do the children notice about the words? Point out the 'medic-' root of this set of words and explain how words that are to do with the same subject often have the same root.

■ Encourage the children to think of other examples. Some suggestions to get them started are: 'dance', 'dancer' and 'dancing'; 'magnet', 'magnetic' and 'magnetism'; 'please' (verb), 'pleasure', 'pleasant', 'pleasing' and 'pleased'.

■ Invite the children to come out and write their own examples on a large sheet of paper. Keep this pinned up and let them add to it at any time. What root gives the longest list of words? Encourage the children to try to beat their own record for the highest number of words from the same root.

■ Write on the board 'TREMORS' from *Play ... If You Dare*. Ask the children to think of words that come from this one. List them. Use a dictionary to discover words derived from the same root and their meanings. You may find 'tremble', 'trembler', 'trembly', 'tremendous', 'tremolo', 'tremulous' and 'trembling poplar'. Invite the children to tell you what the root means (shake or quiver). Explain that the root is 'tremor', from the Latin word 'tremere' meaning 'tremble'.

With the lower-achievers

With adult support

Choose from:

1   Working closely with the children, look again at the examples of word groups that were discussed in the whole-class session. Make sure the children fully understand how the root leads to the creation of other connected words. Help them to write the words, using a different colour for the root.

2   Give the children copies of Resource sheet 6c and help them to make word slides. Ask them how many 'real' words they can make from each root. Help them to use a dictionary to check their words.

3   Together, look through *Play ... If You Dare* for base words and help the children to form other words. For example, 'interested' (page 9) gives 'interest', 'interesting' and 'interestingly'; 'covered' (page 31) gives 'cover', 'covering' and 'coverage'.

Teacher-independent activities

Choose from:

1   Give the children copies of Resource sheet 6c to make and use. They should make the words with the word slide and check with a dictionary how many are 'proper' words.

2   Prepare a set of cards with a root word written on each one. You could use the words discussed in the whole-class session and/or take them from Resource sheet 6c. Make some cards with word endings on them, such as 'er', 'ing', 'ed', 'ful' and 'ous'. Place both packs face down on the table. Play a game where the children take a card from each pile and try to make a new word. If the others agree that it is a 'real' word (by checking in the dictionary, if necessary), the child can take a counter. The winner is the child with the highest number of counters at the end of the game.

3   Working in pairs, ask the children to complete Generic sheet 6 (page 122). Ask them to write words derived from the same root. Encourage them to use a simple dictionary and thesaurus to help them find their words. You could use your own choice of words by blanking off those on the sheet and substituting others.

Plenary session

■ Ask the children who played games to explain to the class what they had to do. Make sure they talk about the 'root' or 'base' of a word.

■ Has anybody discovered a new root giving other words? Encourage the children to write on the large sheet of paper the group of words they found. Did anybody add to the paper after the whole-class session? Let them read out their words.

■ Do all the children understand how several words can be derived from the same root? Are they confident in using a dictionary to check derivations?

TREMORS

47

■ Put a ✔ beside the statements that you think are true.

TREMORS is a series of scary books. ☐

The same character is in all the books. ☐

The books all have a modern setting. ☐

The books all have a happy ending. ☐

TREMORS is a series of books about earthquakes. ☐

There is a different character in every book. ☐

Some of the books are set in the past. ☐

Some of the books have a sad ending. ☐

■ Now complete this sentence.

I like/do not like TREMORS because _____

_____

_____

■ Put these sets of words in order of intensity.

cold	hot	warm

_____ _____ _____

large	small	medium

_____ _____ _____

brave	scared	terrified

_____ _____ _____

beautiful	ugly	pretty

_____ _____ _____

■ Make the word slide and see you how many words you can write.

✂ ----------------------------

er

----

ing

----

ed

----

ful

----

think

jump

wonder

interest

cover

Science fiction stories

Overall aims

- To identify and explore a science fiction setting, using the featured book as a basis for this.

- To understand the use of the apostrophe for possession in the singular form.

- To explore and discuss words which imply gender.

Featured book

Tommy Niner and the Mystery Spaceship by Tony Bradman (Puffin Books, 1995)

Story synopsis

Tommy, Dad and Grandad are about to return to Galactic Council HQ at the end of a mission when they come across the frozen spaceship of Evil Zarella. When the spaceship begins to thaw and Evil Zarella is released from her frozen state, she attacks Tommy's spaceship 'Stardust'. Fierce battles and cosmic space storms all contrive to ensure that the crew of 'Stardust' has a difficult task to defeat the evil spacewoman. But Tommy saves the day and the crew returns home safely with only a few bruises to show for their adventures.

Lesson One

Intended learning

- To identify and explore science fiction settings, using the featured book as a basis for this.

- To discover how the author uses detail to evoke the space setting.

- To be stimulated to discover other science fiction texts.

With the whole class

- Show the cover of *Tommy Niner and the Mystery Spaceship* to the children and ask them what they think the story might be about. Does anybody know the genre? Write 'science fiction' on the board and ask a volunteer to read it. Ask the children to suggest what the story might

include, for example aliens, galactic battles or planet invasions. List their ideas on the board.

- Read the first part of *Tommy Niner and the Mystery Spaceship* to the children. Ask them for words in the text to do with space travel. Write these on the board or let the children come and write them.

- Read the rest of the book and then discuss together some of the incidents, phrases and descriptions that evoke the space setting of the story. For example, Ada, the speaking computer which controls the spaceship's flight, the firing of retro-rockets (page 16), gas clouds and asteroid collisions (page 57) and the Stink Blooms being stimulated by radiation (page 88).

- Look at the list of suggestions that was drawn up at the beginning of the session. How accurate were the children's predictions? Was there anything in *Tommy Niner and the Mystery Spaceship* that wasn't on their list?

- Invite the children to think of other settings that could be used for science fiction stories (not just in space). For example, computers taking over the world, hidden communities in the centre of the Earth, time-machines and time travel, and so on. Encourage them to add their ideas to your list and display the list.

- Do the children think that science fiction stories could be true? Why or why not? Do they think a realistic science fiction story is more exciting than one that is obviously impossible? Why or why not? Look again at the list on the board. What characterises science fiction? Add the children's new suggestions to the list.

With the lower-achievers

With adult support

Choose from:

1   Make sure the children know the elements of a science fiction story. Go through the list on the board with them and discuss together which are in *Tommy Niner and the Mystery Spaceship*. Ask them to write a sentence or two about the elements of science fiction.

2   Using Resource sheet 7a, help the children to complete the sentences about *Tommy Niner and the Mystery Spaceship*.

3 Prepare a set of cards with the title of a book
from the classroom library written on each one.
Make sure there is a selection of science fiction
and other genres. Put the cards and the
corresponding books on the table. Help the
children to match the cards to the books and
then briefly look through each book. They
should decide which are science fiction and
make a display of these. Help them to write a
label for each book saying what type of science
fiction it is. For example, 'Play ... if you dare is
science fiction about a computer game.'

Teacher-independent activities

Choose from:

1 Let the children complete Resource sheet 7a,
working in pairs to support each other.

2 Ask the children to design and draw a 'space
villain' to go into the set of 'space villains' cards
that Tommy is collecting. They should write a
sentence or two about their villain and what
makes them evil.

3 Ask the children to look for other science
fiction stories. They should try to find stories
that have different settings and other themes.
Let them work in pairs to choose one and read
it together. Tell them they will have the
opportunity to tell the others about it in the
plenary session.

Plenary session

■ Has anybody found other non-space science
fiction stories to recommend to the class? Did
anybody discover other space-based stories to
recommend? Ask the children to share these
with the class, saying why they are
recommending them.

■ Let the children who wrote labels to accompany
science fiction books read these to the class.
Encourage the children to explore the science
fiction books at unstructured times.

■ Encourage the children to tell you what
elements make a science fiction story. Look at
the list written in the whole-class session. Does
anything need to be added to this now?

Lesson Two

Intended learning

■ To understand the use of the apostrophe for
possession in the singular form.

■ To use the text as a basis for identifying
the form.

With the whole class

The apostrophe for possession in the plural is dealt
with in the next chapter. Try to avoid introducing
plural owners at this stage.

■ Write on the board the names of some of the
children and one of their possessions. For
example, 'David' and 'book', 'Iqbal' and
'computer' and 'Sarah' and 'tennis ball'. Ask for
volunteers to come and match the owners and
their property. If you need to start them off,
insert an apostrophe + s ('s) between one of the
names and their object. Using a different colour,
circle the 's of each example.

■ Do any of the children know the correct term
for the apostrophe? Write 'apostrophe' on the
board and spend a few moments sounding the
phonemes with the children. Get them to
practise saying it correctly.

■ Explain that we use apostrophe + s for
possession when there is only one owner. Ask if
the children remember the term for 'one'
(singular). Ask for volunteers to come and write
a few examples of singular nouns, for example
'cat', 'car', 'tree' and so on. Ask other children to
write something that these might own. For
example, 'basket', 'engine', 'branches' and so on.
Ask one of the children to match the nouns
with apostrophe + s ('The cat's basket', 'The
car's engine', 'The tree's branches' and so on).

■ Explain that the possessions can be in the plural
('The tree's branches') even when the owner is
singular. Encourage the children to think of
some examples of plural possessions for a
singular owner, for example 'The baby's toys' or
'The boy's football boots'.

■ Look through *Tommy Niner and the Mystery
Spaceship* for examples of singular possessives

with apostrophe + s. For example, Stardust's elderly computer (page 10), Commander Niner's face (page 14), Grandad's sniggers (page 21) and so on.

With the lower-achievers

With adult support

Choose from:

1   Make a set of cards with 's written on them. You will also need a set of noun photo cards (such as those produced by Learning Development Aids – LDA). Place an even number of noun photo cards face down on the table. The children turn over two noun cards and match the nouns in the funniest way they can. They should place an 's card between the two photos and say the ownership aloud. For example, noun cards showing a dog and a car could be 'The dog's car'. Help the children to write down their funny examples.

2   Give the children copies of Resource sheet 7b and ask them to join the owners to their possessions by using apostrophe + s.

3   Ask each child in the group to write their own name in a list on a large sheet of paper. Talk to them about something they own or would like to have. Ask each of them to write 's after their name and then the name of the item they thought of. Can they see how the 's says that the item belongs to them?

Teacher-independent activities

Choose from:

1   Let the children work in pairs or groups of three. Give them a set of noun photo cards (such as those produced by LDA) and a large sheet of paper. Place the noun photo cards face down on the table. The children turn over two cards and match the nouns in the funniest way they can. So if someone picks up the cards 'dog' and 'cat' they can say 'The cat's dog' or 'The dog's cat'. They should write their funny examples on the large sheet of paper. (The nouns could be written in pencil on the back of each card for help with spelling.)

2   Give the children copies of Resource sheet 7b to complete.

3   Start the children off with an alliterative list of possessions, such as Ann's apple, Ben's bike, Cleo's cup and so on. Ask them to add as many more to the list as they can, using a dictionary to help them.

Plenary session

■   Ask the children who made up funny matches and other possessive lists to share them with the class. Did they remember the 's when they wrote them down?

■   Ask the children to remember what 's is called. Make sure they can pronounce 'apostrophe' correctly. Ensure that everybody knows why and how apostrophe + s is used.

Lesson Three

Intended learning

■   To explore and discuss words which imply gender.

■   To use texts to illustrate gender vocabulary.

With the whole class

■   While the children are watching you, write on the board or a large sheet of paper, some of the children's names in two columns, boys and girls. Don't say anything as you do this. Stop after a while and ask one of the children whose name is not on the list to come and write their name in the correct place. Where did they put it? Can the class tell you if they were right or wrong? Discuss how the lists are organised.

■   Ask the children if they know the general terms for gender ('male' and 'female'). Invite a volunteer to write the words on the board, or write them yourself, above the appropriate list of names.

■   Encourage the children to come and write single gender family words in each list. Start them off with 'mum' and 'dad'. They should be able to write 'brother', 'sister', 'aunt', 'uncle', 'grandma' and 'grandad'. Encourage them to think of a gender-free family word ('cousin').

■ Do the children know other words that imply gender? For example, 'fox' and 'vixen' or 'goose' and 'gander'. Add these to the lists. Leave the lists up while working on this lesson. Tell the children that they may add new words to the lists whenever they find some.

■ Tell the children that in most foreign languages, nouns are given a gender. For example, in French and Spanish 'dog' (le chien/el perro) is male, but 'house' (la maison/la casa) is female. Ask children of other ethnic origins whether their languages have similar gender allocations. Invite the children to give you some examples.

■ Explain that in English there are also words that have a gender implication from their endings. For example, 'ess' (princess or actress), 'ette' (usherette or suffragette) or 'a' (Lydia or Hilda). Look at the lists of children's names. Are any of them male/female versions? For example, Daniel and Daniella or Nicholas and Nicola? Point out how the 'a' can feminise a male name. Tell them that this comes from Latin female words, some of which end in 'a'.

■ Ask the children whether they can remember any words in *Tommy Niner and the Mystery Spaceship* which imply gender. They should tell you 'Dad', 'Grandad' and 'Zarella', for example.

With the lower-achievers

With adult support

Choose from:

1 Prepare cards with a word on each which implies gender. (You could use Generic sheet 7 on page 123.) Play a form of 'Pelmanism' where the children have to match the gender pair, for example, duck and drake or lion and lioness. The winner is the child with the highest number of matching pairs.

2 Help the children to read and identify the gender words on Resource sheet 7c. They could use a simple dictionary if necessary. They should then complete the crossword.

3 Help the children to make a large 'Male and Female' poster for the wall. They should either draw or glue pictures of items in gender pairs and label each pair.

4 Prepare cards with a word on each which implies male gender. For example, 'prince', 'tiger' or 'actor'. Give the children a set of letter tiles and then place the cards face down on the table. The children take a card and then make the female word to match each card with their letter tiles. If they are correct they win a token. The winner is the child with the highest number of tokens at the end of the game. This game can also be played in reverse by preparing cards with female gender words.

Teacher-independent activities

Choose from:

1 Let the children complete Resource sheet 7c. Read it through with them before leaving them to do the crossword alone.

2 Prepare a set of cards with a word on each which implies gender (you could use Generic sheet 7 on page 123). Let the children play a form of 'Pelmanism' where they have to match the gender pair. For example, duck and drake or lion and lioness. The winner has the highest number of matching pairs.

3 Give the children copies of a simple text that has a lot of gender words in it. They should identify and reverse the gender words which might provide a humorous result! 'Little Master Muffet sat on his tuffet' or 'Jackie Spratt could eat no fat, her husband could eat no lean.'

Plenary session

■ Did anybody find new gender words and add them to the list? Let them come out and show the class which words. What do the words mean?

■ Does everybody understand the terms 'female, 'male' and 'gender'? Ask for a volunteer to give you examples of male and female partner words, for example 'actor' and 'actress'. Let them write their words on the board.

Name _____

■ Finish these sentences. Use the words in the word box to help you.

science fiction	spaceship	gas clouds
galactic	asteroids	space	retro-rocket
planets	mystery	radiation

'Tommy Niner and the Mystery Spaceship' is a _____

_____ story. It is set in _____

I know this because there are _____

_____

_____ in the story.

✎ Draw a picture of Tommy Niner or Evil Zarella.

■ Look at this picture. Who owns what?

■ Write down who owns each thing. Remember to use 's.
The first one has been done for you.

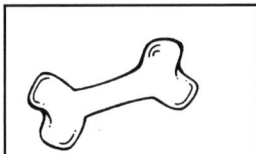   The dog's bone. _____

   _____

   _____

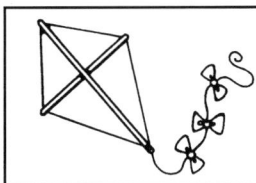   _____

Name _____

■ Read these words.

vixen	fox	man	king	woman
doe	hen	cock	duck	gander
	aunt	cob	actor	

■ If there are some words you don't know, find them in a dictionary.

■ Now do the crossword – all the answers are the words at the top of the sheet.

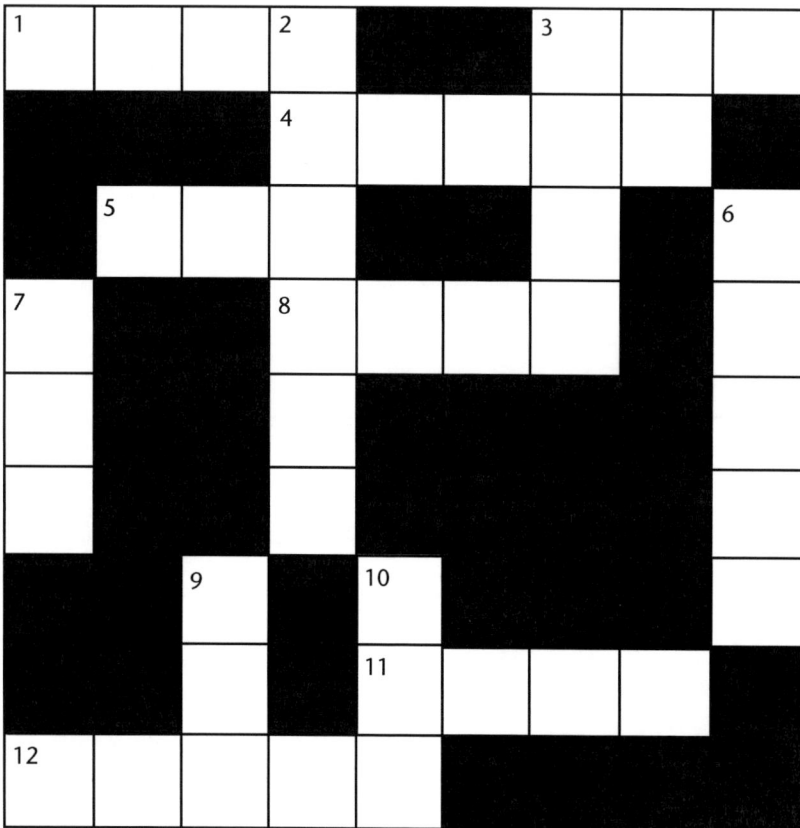

ACROSS

1 A male ruler (k _ _ _)

3 A male swan (c _ _)

4 A man in films (a _ _ _ _)

5 A female bird (h _ _)

8 You might find this female bird in a pond (d _ _ _)

11 A female relative (a _ _ _)

12 A female fox (v _ _ _ _)

DOWN

2 A male goose (g _ _ _ _ _)

3 A male bird (c _ _ _)

6 A female person (w _ _ _ _)

7 A female rabbit or deer (d _ _)

9 A vixen's mate (f _ _)

10 A male person (m _ _)

Fantasy stories

Overall aims

- To explore fantasy stories and discuss what differentiates these from other types of story.
- To understand the use of the apostrophe for possession in the plural form.
- To explore a range of suffixes that can be added to nouns and verbs to make adjectives.

Featured book

Lionheart by Lynne Markham (Mammoth, 1998)

Story synopsis

When Leo visits his grandfather in the country, he feels a strange tie to the stuffed lion in the study. When he touches it, golden sparks fly and Leo's hand tingles and buzzes. He then finds himself on the African plains experiencing the same feelings as a lion. In fact, he is a lion! He is sure that his grandfather knows about this and can explain the mystery. In time, that is what happens and Grandfather tells Leo how his father unwillingly shot the lion, but now its spirit lives on in the family's male line. Eventually, the lion's heart will enter Leo, giving him the strength and gentleness that are to be found in the king of the jungle.

Lesson One

Intended learning

- To explore fantasy stories and discuss what differentiates these from other types of story.
- To use the featured text as a stimulus for discussing fantasy stories.
- To be motivated to discover other fantasy stories.

With the whole class

- Ask the children if they know what 'fantasy' means. Write on the board some key words, for example, 'imaginary', 'unreal', 'legend', 'myth' and so on. What might a fantasy story be about? Have they read any fantasy stories?

Write the titles on the board. Leave these up while working on this lesson.

- Discuss what elements are in a fantasy story. For example, the setting (in an imaginary land), the characters (either unreal people or animals that speak) or the events (impossible happenings and incidents). Look at the titles suggested by the children at the beginning of the session and explore why these books are fantasy stories. How do they fit the elements discussed?

- Show them the cover of *Lionheart* and ask what they think the story might be about. Read the blurb on the back. Discuss some ideas about the mystery of the dead lion.

- Read *Lionheart*, stopping at appropriate points (the end of Chapters 2, 3 and 5) to discuss the story together. Why is Leo so drawn to the stuffed lion? What makes the golden sparks come from it? What could be the special bond between Leo and his grandfather? Could Leo really be in Africa? Has anybody any ideas about the truth of the mystery?

- Finish reading the book. What is it that makes *Lionheart* a fantasy story? Could the story have really happened? Why not? Look at the key words and ideas that were written at the beginning of the session. How does *Lionheart* fit in with these?

With the lower-achievers

With adult support

Choose from:

1   Make sure the children understand the elements of a fantasy story. Discuss some of the elements of a fantasy story again: imaginary places, people or animals with unusual abilities, and impossible happenings. Discuss *Lionheart*. What makes it a fantasy story? Together list the key points that make it a fantasy story. Do the children like fantasy stories? Invite them to give reasons for their answers.

2   Give the children copies of Resource sheet 8a. They should tick the books that are fantasy stories. Give reading support if necessary. Help them to complete the sentence about *Lionheart* using the words at the bottom of the sheet.

3   Look at some other fantasy stories together and discuss what makes them fantasy stories. You could start with some fairytales. For example, 'Jack and the Beanstalk' has a fantasy setting (the giant's home), with a giant (an imaginary character) and impossible happenings (the beanstalk growing up to the sky in one night). Give out copies of Generic sheet 8 (page 124) and help the children to put the elements of the story into the correct sections. They should then add other stories to the sections.

Teacher-independent activities

Choose from:

1   Give the children a small selection of stories, one or two fantasy and one or two 'realistic'. Ask them to work in pairs to decide which are the fantasy stories. They should discuss setting, character and events. Ask them to write or tape record why they made their decisions.

2   Give the children copies of Resource sheet 8a to complete. You may need to read it with them first.

3   Let the children work in pairs and give them a comic. Ask them to look at the strips and decide together which are fantasy and which could be real. They should write the names of the strips which are fantasy. Can they also write why they decided this? They could use Generic sheet 8 (page 124) to record their thoughts.

Plenary session

■   Ask the children who discussed the selection of fantasy stories to share these with the class by either reading what they wrote or playing their cassette.

■   Let the children who completed a resource or generic sheet explain to the others what they did.

■   What are the characteristics of a fantasy story? Look again at the ideas written on the board at the whole-class session and check that everybody understands them.

Lesson Two

Intended learning

■   To understand the use of the apostrophe for possession in the plural form.

■   To use the text as a basis for identifying the form.

With the whole class

■   Write on the board a list of nouns in the plural, ensuring they are regular – for example, 'boys', 'dogs', 'cars' and 'coats'. Ask the children what they have in common (they are plurals). Spend a few moments revising plurals if necessary.

■   Ask the children to suggest possessions for some plural owners, such as 'football boots', 'bones', 'horns' and 'buttons'. Let them come and write their suggestions beside the owners.

■   Do the children remember how to show possession? (If they say *"By putting apostrophe s"*, accept the answer but remind them that 'apostrophe s' is for an owner in the singular.) Encourage the children to use the correct term. Write 'apostrophe' on the board.

■   Explain to the children that when there is more than one owner, we use the apostrophe only. This is because the noun already ends in 's' to show the plural. Using a different colour, fill in the apostrophe beside each noun – 'boys' football boots', 'dogs' bones', 'cars' horns' and 'coats' buttons'. Ask the children for some other examples of plural owners and their possessions. Encourage them to write these on the board, not forgetting the apostrophe.

■   Look at page 58 of *Lionheart* for the example 'vultures' wings'. Show it to the children and ask them whether there is one vulture or more. How do they know? (At this stage, do not introduce irregular plurals such as 'men', 'children' or 'people'.)

■   Tell the children that plural owners might share a single possession. For example, the teachers' staffroom or the boys' computer. Ask for some more examples of plural owners and single possessions. Let the children write these on the board, with the apostrophe.

With the lower-achievers

With adult support

Choose from:

1   Prepare a set of cards with plural owners (without an apostrophe) written on each – for example, 'girls', 'dogs', 'doors' and 'cars'. Use a set of noun photo cards such as those produced by LDA to play a game. The two sets of cards are placed face down on the table. The children take one of each and try to match them. They should try to make the match as silly as possible, for example 'the dogs' cars'. Help them to write their matches, making sure they put the apostrophe after the owners.

2   Give the children copies of Resource sheet 8b. They should join the owners and the possessions. Give reading help if necessary. Help them to write some sentences on the back of the sheet using the examples.

3   Prepare a set of cards with plural owners (without an apostrophe) written on each, for example 'boys', 'birds' and 'jars'. Place the cards face down on the table. The children take one and suggest something that the owners might have, for example, 'footballs', 'nests' and 'lids'. Help the children to write the owners and the possessions using the apostrophe.

Teacher-independent activities

Choose from:

1   Prepare two sets of cards: one with a plural noun written on each and the other with an apostrophe on each. There should be twice as many noun cards as apostrophe cards. Place the cards face down on the table in their separate piles. The children take two noun cards and one apostrophe card. They should match the cards to make owners and their possessions, putting the apostrophe card in the right place. They should then write their matches.

2   Give the children copies of Resource sheet 8b to complete. Tell them that when they have

finished they should write two or three sentences for some of the examples.

3   Prepare Generic sheet 4 (page 120) by writing plural owners in each left shoe, such as 'the birds' and 'the cats'. The children should think of and write the possessions in the right shoe and the correct apostrophe after the names of the owners. You could challenge them to make the phrases alliterative, such as 'the birds' beaks' and 'the cats' claws'.

Plenary session

■   Before the session write on the board some plural owners without an apostrophe. You could use Resource sheet 8b. Ask for volunteers to come and write a possession for each and the apostrophe in the correct place.

■   Is there anything the children find difficult about using the apostrophe for plural owners? Does everybody understand that only an apostrophe is added? Ask them to tell you why.

■   Play a game where you give a plural owner and the children have to think of a possession that starts with the same letter. Then choose a child to think of a plural owner and you have to think of a possession that starts with the same letter. Write them on the board as they are said.

Lesson Three

Intended learning

■   To explore a range of suffixes that can be added to nouns and verbs to make adjectives.

■   To use the featured text to identify these suffixes.

With the whole class

■   Write 'suffix' on the board. Ask the children to read it and tell you what it means. Invite some examples. If necessary, add to the list 'ful', 'able' and 'less'.

- Challenge the children to think of nouns or verbs that can go in front of these suffixes to make adjectives. For example, 'play' and 'ful' make 'playful', or 'hat' and 'less' make 'hatless'.

- Play 'Suffix Sense and Nonsense'. For example, you say *"Rashid, is this sense or nonsense: 'wishless'?"* or *"Annie, is this sense or nonsense: 'eatable'?"* Let the children take turns to ask each other.

- Talk about how the words are no longer a noun or a verb because adding the suffix has changed them. They have become adjectives, words that describe a noun. So adding 'less' to 'water' makes an adjective that describes a place.

- Look in *Lionheart* for examples of words with these suffixes. There is 'powerful' (page 18), 'shadeless' (page 27), 'sleepless' (page 49), 'watchful' (page 55) and 'fretful' (page 62). Discuss with the children what each of these means. Ask for volunteers to write each one on the board and circle the suffix with a different colour.

- Point out to the children that there is only one 'l' in the suffix 'ful'. Ask for some more examples of words with 'ful'. Let them write them on the board, making sure they put only one 'l'. You might also need to point out that sometimes when you add a suffix the spelling of the root word changes, such as in 'beautiful'.

With the lower-achievers

With adult support

Choose from:

1   Using Resource sheet 8c, help the children to match the words to the appropriate suffixes to make adjectives. Help them to write a sentence for some of the adjectives they make.

2   Look through some other texts with the children to find further examples of nouns and verbs to make adjectives with the suffixes being explored ('ful', 'able' and 'less'). Help the children to write the new adjectives. They should write the suffix in a different colour.

3   Prepare Generic sheet 1 (page 117) with a noun or a verb in alternate 'bricks'. Help the children to make an adjective from each of these by

adding one of the suffixes. They should write the new adjective in the same 'brick'.

Teacher-independent activities

Choose from:

1   Let the children complete Resource sheet 8c. Challenge them to write sentences for some of the adjectives.

2   Prepare a set of cards with a noun or a verb written on each and write each suffix on a sheet of paper as a memory aid. Let the children play a game by placing the cards face down on the table. Each child takes a card, reads the word and makes an adjective by adding one of the suffixes. If the others agree that it is correct, the child wins a token. The winner is the child with the most tokens at the end of the game.

3   Prepare inflated balloons with a different suffix on each. Give the children a list of nouns and verbs and a set of 'tail papers'. Ask them to write on each 'tail paper' an adjective made from the noun/verb list and one of the suffixes. Attach the 'tail papers' to string and tie them to the relevant balloon. Suspend them from the ceiling.

Plenary session

- Before the session, write on the board some nouns and verbs and the suffixes. Ask for volunteers to make adjectives by adding one of the suffixes. Have the children remembered to put only one 'l' when writing 'ful'?

- Let the children who completed the resource sheet or made balloon tails explain to the others what they did. Ask the children to tell you what a suffix is.

- What did the children enjoy about this lesson? Was there anything they found difficult? Do they understand how the suffix creates an adjective from a noun or a verb?

■ Put a tick (✓) beside the books that could be fantasy stories.

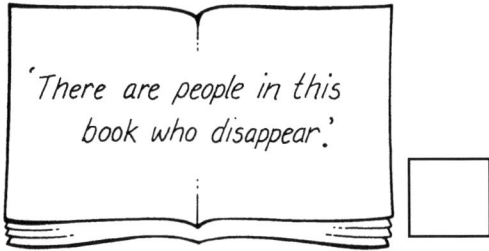

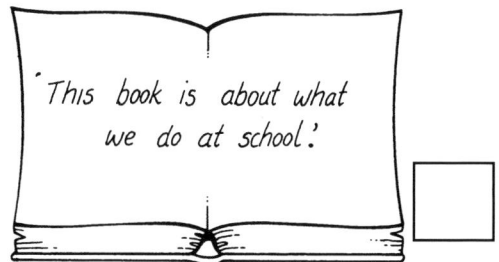

'This story is set in the clouds.' ☐

'This story is about a little boy called Sam.' ☐

'There are people in this book who disappear.' ☐

'This story is set in America.' ☐

'This story is about a dog that can talk and fly.' ☐

'This book is about what we do at school.' ☐

■ Complete the sentence. You can use the words at the bottom of the sheet to help you.

'Lionheart' is a fantasy story because _____

_____

_____

Leo   Africa   animal   imaginary

                 unreal   impossible

Name _____

■ Use an apostrophe to join the owners and their possessions.
One has been done for you.

cars

tyres

the cars' tyres

boys

footballs

birds

nests

jars

lids

girls

gloves

■ Read these **suffixes**.

ful   ing   less   able

■ Draw a line from the suffixes to the words
to make some adjectives. Some of the
words can use more than one suffix.

power

wear

help

shock

watch

fear

ing

ful

able

less

Poems from other cultures

Overall aims

- To explore poems from different cultures.
- To explore rhyme and verse patterns in poetry.
- To explore rhythm and line patterns in poetry.
- To use poems from different cultures as a stimulus to write own poetry.

Featured books

Another Second Poetry Book, compiled by John Foster (Oxford University Press, 1988)

Let's Celebrate Festival Poems, compiled by John Foster (Oxford University Press, 1989)

Lesson One

Chosen poem

'Chicken Dinner' by Valerie Bloom, page 67

Intended learning

- To discuss how the poem has been influenced by Caribbean culture.
- To explore the rhyme, line and verse patterns of the poem.

With the whole class

- Enlarge a copy of 'Chicken Dinner'. Read the title to the children and ask them what they think the poem is about. What do they think of when they hear the phrase 'Chicken Dinner'?

- Share the poem with the children, letting them follow the text. Were they right in their ideas as to what the poem is about? Were they glad that Henrietta escaped? How did the child in the poem feel at the end? Was it the sort of chicken dinner they had expected?

- Do the children think the poem is set in Britain? Can they say why or why not? Can they tell you where it might be set? Explain that it comes from the Caribbean and there are clues in the text that show us this. Some of the following ideas can be discussed: the dialect

used; words such as 'fe' for 'for', 'yuh' for 'you', 'dat' for 'that', 'Don' used without the final 't'; grammatical examples such as 'We know dat chicken from she hatch' and 'Yuh promise her to we as a pet'; the reference to a mongoose, an animal not found in Britain.

- Look at a globe or atlas and find the Caribbean. Show the distance between Britain and the Caribbean. Explain that many people came to live in Britain from the Caribbean in the 1950s and 1960s. If there are children in the class of Caribbean background, encourage them to share some of their experiences and customs with the other children.

- Look again at the poem and discuss its rhyme and verse patterns. How many verses are there? How many lines in each verse? Is the verse pattern regular? How is it different in verse 4? Is the line pattern regular? What do the children notice about lines 2 and 6 of each verse? What can they tell you about the last line of each verse? What is the rhyme pattern? What are the rhyming words in each verse?

With the lower-achievers

With adult support

Choose from:

1   Read the poem again with the children, encouraging them to join in. Discuss together the dialect and look for more examples, such as 'de' for 'the' and 'ah' for 'I'. Look at the different grammar, such as 'Mama, me really glad, yuh know' and 'me suddenly feel upset,/Yuh don' suppose is somebody pet/We eating now fe dinner?' Talk about practical differences such as the idea of keeping chickens for eggs (where do most of us get eggs?) or the mother in the poem killing the chicken herself (where do we get chickens for dinner?). Explain here that not all Caribbean families keep chickens for eggs and dinner. Tell the children that the mongoose is an animal found in Africa. Discuss the fact that the chicken had escaped the mongoose's raids. In this country it is the fox that raids the chickens' coop. Did the children enjoy the poem? Can they say why or why not? Help them to write a few sentences about their feelings for the child and the chicken.

2 Make sure the children understand the ideas explored in the whole-class session about the verse, line and rhyme pattern of the poem. If necessary, share the poem once more, covering the teaching points again. Let them write the rhyming words on the board.

3 Give the children copies of Resource sheet 9a and help them to complete each section about 'Chicken Dinner'.

4 Explore together some other poems by black poets such as Benjamin Zephaniah, Grace Nichols or John Agard and discuss how Caribbean culture is embedded in and influences their poetry.

5 Arrange a visit to school by somebody from the Caribbean (perhaps a parent or grandparent of one of the children) who could tell the children what life in the Caribbean is like. Ask them to share some poetry, stories and songs with the children.

Teacher-independent activities

Choose from:

1 Give the children copies of Resource sheet 9a to complete. You may need to read it with them before letting them work independently.

2 Ask the children to write a story about Henrietta the chicken and how she escaped becoming a dinner.

3 Let the children work as a group and give them an anthology containing poems by Caribbean writers. (For example, *The Puffin Book of Utterly Brilliant Poetry*.) Ask them to choose one of the poems that they think has been influenced by Caribbean culture and to come to the plenary session ready to tell the others why they think this is.

Plenary session

■ Can anybody tell you about the rhyme, line and verse patterns of 'Chicken Dinner'? Ask for volunteers to explain how we know the poem is from the Caribbean.

■ Let the children who wrote a story about Henrietta read it to the class.

■ Ask the group that found a Caribbean poem to explain to the others how the poem gives us clues as to how it has been influenced by Caribbean culture.

Lesson Two

Chosen poem

'Lion Dance' by Trevor Millum page 68

Intended learning

■ To explore how the poem is about a Chinese festival.

■ To identify the rhythm and rhyme patterns of the poem.

■ To use poems from different cultures as a stimulus to write own poetry.

With the whole class

■ Enlarge a copy of 'Lion Dance'. Read the title to the children and ask them what they think the poem might be about. Can they tell you which culture it is from? Explain that it is about the Lion Dance which is performed at the Chinese New Year. Tell them that the lion is made up of a long line of men underneath a very colourful costume that represents a lion. (Sometimes it is a dragon.) The lion dances through the streets to the very noisy accompaniment of many percussion instruments, such as cymbals, drums and gongs. The onlookers follow and join in with the dance. If there are children in the class from a Chinese background, encourage them to share with the class their experiences of the New Year celebrations, including the Lion Dance.

■ Share the poem with the children letting them follow the text. Can anybody suggest what the words in the poem represent? Is it easy to imagine the sound of the percussion from the words used? Why are words such as 'clash', 'gong' and 'clang' used? Is the rhythm of the poem regular? Why not? (It represents the irregular playing of the instruments and movements of the lion.) Is there a rhyme pattern? Is it regular? What are the rhyming words? What words and phrases express the different movements, gestures and moods of the lion? How are louder noises and more frenzied dancing expressed? (With the use of exclamation marks at the ends of some of the lines.) Does anybody know what 'Gong she fah chai' means? ('Happy New Year' in Mandarin.)

■ As a class make up more lines to add to the poem. Brainstorm words that express the noise of the percussion and the movements of the lion. For example, 'boom', 'dong', 'tish', 'lion twist', 'lion spin' and 'lion spring'. Together, decide on the lines and add them to the bottom of the enlarged copy. Leave it up for reference during the group session.

With the lower-achievers

With adult support

Choose from:

1 Share the poem again with the children. Allocate one or two lines to each child (or a pair) and help them to learn their lines, encouraging them to use volume and expression to convey the atmosphere of the poem. Put the lines together, with you reciting the 'leftovers', to perform the complete poem.

2 Give out Resource sheet 9b. The children should cut out the words and arrange them on another sheet of paper to make a poem of their own, based on 'Lion Dance'. Give help where necessary.

3 Give the children copies of Resource sheet 9c. Help them to match the rhyming words from 'Lion Dance' and then find others for each set. They should then write a short poem about the percussion instruments in 'Lion Dance'. Give support if necessary.

4 Look at books together about Chinese culture. Arrange a visit to school by somebody from China or Hong Kong (perhaps a parent or grandparent of one of the children) who could tell the children what life there is like.
Ask them to share some poems or songs with the children.

Teacher-independent activities

Choose from:

1 Give the children copies of Resource sheet 9b to complete. Read it through with them first then explain that they have to cut out the words and use them to create a poem of their own based on 'Lion Dance'. When they are happy with their poem they should stick the words in order on another sheet of paper. They could illustrate their poems.

2 Challenge the children to work in pairs and write a short poem about a British celebration or festival, such a Bonfire Night or Christmas.

3 Give the children copies of Resource sheet 9c to complete. They could work in pairs for this activity.

Plenary session

■ Let the children who learned the poem (or parts of it with you) give a class performance.

■ Ask the children who completed Resource sheet 9b to read their Lion Dance poems to the class.

■ What did the children learn about the rhythm pattern of 'Lion Dance'? What can they tell you about its rhyme pattern?

Chicken Dinner

Mama, don' do it, please
Don' cook dat chicken fe
    dinner,
We know dat chicken from
    she hatch,
She is de only one in de
    batch
Dat mongoose didn' catch,
Don' bother cook her fe
    dinner.

Mama, don' do it, please
Don' cook dat chicken fe
    dinner,
Yuh mean to tell mi yuh feget
Yuh promise her to we as a
    pet
She not even have a chance
    to lay yet
An yuh going to cook her fe
    dinner?

Mama, don' do it, please
Don' cook dat chicken fe
    dinner,
Don' give Henrietta de chop,
Ah tell yuh what, we could
    swop,
We could get yuh another
    one from de shop,
If yuh promise not to cook
    her fe dinner.

Mama, me really glad, yuh
    know,
Yuh never cook Henny fe
    dinner,
An she glad too, ah bet,
Oh gosh, me suddenly feel
    upset,
Yuh don' suppose is
    somebody pet
We eating now fe dinner?

Valerie Bloom

Lion Dance

Drum drum gong drum
gong gong cymbal gong
gong she fah chai
cymbal clang drum clash
gong she fah chai
lion saunter lion strut
gong-she gong-she
yellow body bright eye
gong she fah chai
eye wink eye flash
cymbal clang drum clash
lion coy lion cute
she-she she-she
lion lie lion sleep
fah chai fah chai
fah chai fah chai
gong she fah chai
man walk man creep
gong she fah chai
lion wake! Lion leap!
gong she fah chai!
lion angry lion cross
gong-gong she-she fah-fah chai-chai
lion leap lion high
chai! chai! chai! chai!
people cower people fly
gong chai! gong chai!
lion pounce lion prance!
gong gong gong gong gong gong gong gong
gong she fah chai!
gong gong gong gong gong gong gong gong
GONG SHE LION DANCE!!
GONG SHE LION DANCE!!

Trevor Millum

■ Read 'Chicken Dinner' and then cross out the wrong answers.

'Chicken Dinner' is set in Britain/the Caribbean.

The chicken in the poem is called Valerie/Henrietta.

A mongoose/fox killed the other chickens.

■ Write the rhyming words from 'Chicken Dinner' in their verse order.

1 _____   catch   pet   2 _____

_____   batch   _____
                                              yet
_____   feget   _____
                              upset

                      swop   bet
3 _____   hatch   4 _____

_____   chop   shop   _____

_____   pet   _____

■ Use the words below to help you write about the verse pattern of 'Chicken Dinner'.

_____

_____

regular   six   rhyme   four   pattern   lines

■ Cut out the words below. Use them to make a
poem about the Lion Dance. Then compare your
poem with a friend's.

boom	people	goes	leaps
clap	the	lion	boom
drum	and	and	clash
the	cymbals	the	clap
the	crash	dance	gong

■ Match the rhyming words from 'Lion Dance'.

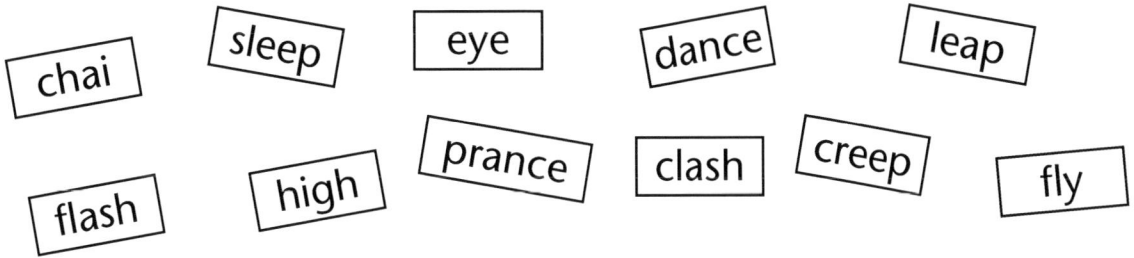

chai   sleep   eye   dance   leap

flash   high   prance   clash   creep   fly

■ Find two more rhyming words for each group.

clash	high	dance	leap

■ Use the words in the box below to help you write a short poem about the percussion instruments in 'Lion Dance'.

Boom, bang, crash, drum _____

Cymbal _____

Tish, ting _____

Gong _____

_____

clang	zing	clash	chai	bong	flash

Poems with different patterns

Overall aims

- To read and compare two poems which have different patterns of rhyme and verse.

- To be able to explore other poetry with different patterns.

- To use the chosen poems as a basis for writing own poetry.

Lesson One

Chosen poem

'Minibeasts' by Mike Jubb, page 75

Intended learning

- To explore the subject matter of the chosen poem.

- To identify the rhyming pattern in the poem.

- To explore the verse structure of the poem.

With the whole class

- Enlarge a copy of the poem 'Minibeasts'. Tell the children that they are going to explore some poems with different patterns of rhyme and verse in them.

- Read the title of the poem and ask the children what they think it might be about. Ask them to name some minibeasts. Let them write their suggestions on the board themselves.

- Read the poem to the children, letting them follow the text. What is the poem about? Ask the children to name some of the minibeasts in the poem. How many of the minibeasts are on the list the children wrote before they heard the poem? Which did they leave out? Write these on the board. Ask the children to share anything they know about any of them.

- Look again at the poem and ask the children to look for the rhyming words. Can they remember what rhyming means? Let them come and point to the rhymes in the poem. For example 'term'/'worms', 'squeeze'/'trees', 'ditch'/'which' and so on.

- Tell the children that the rhyming pattern of the poem is a a, b b , c c and so on. Use the actual terms here, as they will need to learn about this 'a b c' format. Ask if any of them remember the term for rhymes that follow in successive lines (rhyming couplets). Read the poem again with the children, encouraging them to supply the rhyming couplets for each verse.

- Tell the children that now they are going to look at the pattern of verses in the poem. Do they know what a verse is? Ask them how many verses there are in the poem and how many lines in the verses (one of 14 lines, three of 2 lines and one of 4 lines). Challenge them to say whether the poem has a regular or irregular verse pattern (irregular). Encourage them to say how they know. Explain that poetry does not always need a regular pattern of verses and lines.

With the lower-achievers

With adult support

Choose from:

1   Look at the poem again. Discuss the rhyming couplets and the pattern of verses. Make sure the children understand the terms 'rhyme', 'couplet' and 'verse'. Choose two or three of the rhyming couplets and encourage the children to find other words that rhyme with them. For example, 'term'/'worms' could have 'squirm' or 'squeeze'/'trees' could have 'breeze'. Working with a rhyming dictionary on this activity would be fun.

2   Give the children copies of Resource sheet 10a to complete. Give reading support where necessary.

3   Explore together the rhyme and verse patterns of some other poetry. You could use nursery rhymes or let the children choose their favourite poems from a class anthology. Ask them to identify the rhymes and the verses of each poem.

4   Look at books about minibeasts and find some (or all) of the ones in the poem. Read about these with the children. Help them to write a few sentences about their favourite minibeast.

Teacher-independent activities

Choose from:

1 Using Generic sheet 1 (page 117), ask the children to write in each 'brick' of the word wall the rhyming couplets of 'Minibeasts'. Let them use the enlarged copy for reference.

2 Give pairs of children copies of Resource sheet 10a to complete. You may need to read it through with them first.

3 Give the children a well-known poem or rhyme, such as 'One, two, three, four, five, Once I caught a fish alive...' or 'Hickory Dickory Dock'. Ask them to substitute some of the words in the poems but keep the rhyming couplets, for example, 'Once I caught some bees in a hive...' or 'The mouse ran in my sock...' Tell them it is important to find rhyming words first before putting the verses together.

Plenary session

■ Write 'couplet' on the board. Ask what it means. Using the enlarged copy of the poem as reference, ask the children to give you some examples of couplets from 'Minibeasts'. Did any of them find examples of other rhymes with couplets? Share these with the class.

■ Together, write a new version of 'One, two, three, four, five, Once I caught a fish alive...' or 'Hickory Dickory Dock', substituting new words for the rhyming ones.

Lesson Two

Chosen poem
'A waste of time' by Mike Jubb, page 76

Intended learning
■ To identify the rhyming pattern in the poem.
■ To explore the verse structure of the poem.
■ To be able to explore other poetry with different patterns.
■ To use the chosen poems as a basis for writing own poetry.

With the whole class
■ Enlarge a copy of 'A waste of time'. Tell the children they are going to explore a poem by the same poet who wrote 'Minibeasts'.

■ Read the poem with the children and ask them what it is about. Talk about how it would be a waste of time to try to stop the wind from blowing or the rain from falling. Can they think of any other examples of what would be a waste of time? For example, trying to stop dogs barking, cats miaowing and birds singing.

■ Do the children notice anything about the last two lines of the poem? Invite them to suggest why the poet chose to separate them rather than continue the rhyming pattern within the same verse.

■ Ask for volunteers to identify the rhyming words in the poem. What is its rhyming pattern? Explain that it has rhymes on alternate lines. Invite the children to explain what 'alternate' means or explain it to the class. Ask for volunteers to come out and point to the alternate line rhymes.

■ What do the children notice about the beginning of every line? (They all start with the word 'telling'.) Why is this? Ask them what is different about the rhyming pattern of this poem when compared with 'Minibeasts'. Remind them that 'Minibeasts' had rhyming couplets. Read the poem again with the children, encouraging them to supply the rhyming words.

■ Tell the children that now they are going to look at the pattern of verses in the poem. How many verses are there in the poem? Ask them to count the lines in each verse (there is one of 14 lines and one of 2 lines). Do the children think this is a regular or an irregular verse pattern? Why? This poem, like 'Minibeasts', has an irregular verse pattern, but it is very different.

With the lower-achievers

With adult support

Choose from:

1 Look at the poem again together. Discuss the rhyming pattern of alternate lines and the pattern of verses. Ask the children to tell you which are their favourite lines. Encourage them to explain why. Help them to make up another line that rhymes with their favourite line. They could then write their own rhyme, their favourite line and the other two lines of the quartet. For example, if 'Telling frogs not to hop' is their favourite, they could decide on 'Telling cars not to stop' as a rhyming line and then write,

> Telling birds not to fly
> Telling frogs not to hop
> Telling babies not to cry
> Telling cars not to stop.

2 Give the children copies of Resource sheet 10b and help them to complete each of the sentences about the rhyme and verse patterns of 'A waste of time'. Give reading support where necessary.

3 Read both chosen poems again with the children. Which is their favourite? Encourage them to give reasons for their responses. Let them choose a line from one of the poems. Help them to learn it and then recite it in role. For example, if they choose 'Spiders spinning silky nets', they could move their hands and legs to suggest the spinning of the web.

4 Using Resource sheet 10c, help the children to complete the poem about minibeasts. Let them see the enlarged copy of 'Minibeasts' for

support. You could provide a rhyming dictionary to help them.

Teacher-independent activities

Choose from:

1 Give pairs of children copies of Resource sheet 10b to complete.

2 Ask the children to work in pairs to choose two lines from 'A waste of time'. Challenge them to write new rhyming words for the final words of each of the two lines. They should list as many as possible.

3 Let the children complete Resource sheet 10c. They could work in pairs to produce a joint poem if preferred.

Plenary session

■ Discuss other ideas for lines that could be added to 'A waste of time' – for example, 'Telling flowers not to grow' or 'Telling cats not to purr'. Add some to the poem, continuing the rhyming pattern if possible.

■ Ask the children who learned lines in role from the poems to recite them to the class. Why did they choose their lines?

■ Ask the children who wrote their own poems to read or recite them to the other children.

■ Ask the class which of the two poems is their favourite and why.

Minibeasts

Creatures of the summer term:
Sliding slugs and wiggling worms;
Spiders spinning silky nets,
Crickets playing castanets;
Woodlice in their armour squeeze
Under stones and fallen trees,
While millipedes and centipedes
Scurry round at such a speed,
Up the bank and down the ditch;
Tell me which leg follows which.
And as they're busy counting feet,
The caterpillar has to eat
And eat and eat because she must
Get fat until she's fit to bust.

There's ants and ladybirds, and snails
That leave their silvery trails,

There's butterflies we all admire,
And dragonflies that don't breathe fire.

Yellow and black can signal 'Danger',
So treat the wasp just like a stranger.

There's beetles, bugs and busy bees,
And many, many more than these.
They run and fly, they hop and squirm,
These creatures of the summer term.

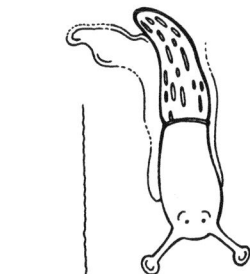

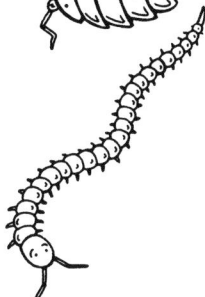

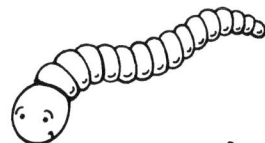

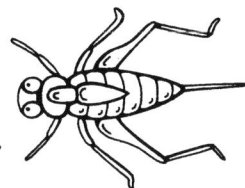

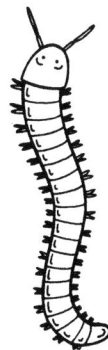

Mike Jubb

A waste of time

Telling the wind not to blow
Telling the tide not to turn
Telling a river not to flow
Telling fire not to burn
Telling birds not to fly
Telling frogs not to hop
Telling babies not to cry
Telling bubbles not to pop
Telling rain not to fall
Telling lightning not to flash
Telling cuckoos not to call
Telling water not to splash
Telling dogs not to wag
Telling the sun not to shine

Telling parents not to nag
Telling children not to whine

Mike Jubb

■ Read 'Minibeasts' again and then complete the following sentences. You can use words from the box below to help you.

| couplets | verse | lines | rhyme | irregular |

The rhymes in 'Minibeasts' are in _____

There are _____ verses in 'Minibeasts'.

The first verse has _____ lines.

_____ have two lines.

There are _____ lines in the last verse.

The verse pattern is _____

■ Now look at this poem. Underline the rhyming couplets in different colours.

I have a friend called Fred
Who has the weirdest head!
He's got sticky-up hair
Like a prickly pear.
And sticky-out ears
Like jugs of beer!

■ How many verses are there in this poem? _____
■ How many lines are there in the poem? _____

■ Read 'A waste of time' and then finish these sentences.
  You can use the words in the box to help you.

| alternate   verses   lines   rhyme   irregular |

There are two _____ in 'A waste of time'.

The first verse has _____ lines.

The second _____ has two lines.

The verse pattern is _____

The rhymes are on _____ lines.

■ Now write some of the rhyming words in the poem.

_____ and _____

_____ and _____

_____ and _____

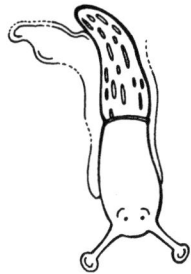

■ Complete this poem about minibeasts.
Try to make the lines rhyme.

I'm sitting here on the garden wall
Watching minibeasts creep and _____
I wonder what they do all day.
Do they eat or sleep or talk or _____?

I see a snail with a shiny shell
And there's a caterpillar _____
I like the bee buzzing here and there
And the ladybirds are _____

The worms just love to slither and slide.
The slugs like to use my dustbin to _____
The butterfly does such a dainty dance
Will she land on my hand – no _____!

■ Now try to write two lines of your own about minibeasts.
Use a rhyming dictionary to help you.

_____

_____

Stories that raise issues

Overall aims

- To identify the social issues raised in the featured text.

- To use the text as a stimulus to explore other texts which raise social, moral or cultural issues.

- To understand how grammar alters when the sentence type is altered.

- To spell words by analogy to other known words.

Featured book

How To Write Really Badly by Anne Fine (Mammoth, 1996)

Story synopsis

Chester Howard, an American boy, arrives at his new school in England and knows instantly that he is going to hate it. This is confirmed when Miss Tate makes Chester sit beside Joe Gardener, who thinks he is no good at anything. Chester can hardly believe his eyes when he sees how badly Joe writes, or how much trouble Joe has with anything 'academic'. A remarkable relationship develops between the two boys, with Chester helping Joe to realise that everybody has something they are good at, and Joe helping Chester realise that, deep down, he is actually capable of caring about people.

Lesson One

Intended learning

- To identify the social issues raised in the featured text.

- To use the text as a stimulus to explore other texts which raise social, moral or cultural issues.

With the whole class

This lesson may take several sessions.

- Display the front cover of *How To Write Really Badly* and ask the children what they think this story might be about. Point to the facial expressions of the characters. Ask the children to suggest what they might be thinking or feeling. What does the title of the book suggest to them? Could it mean, for example, that the book is a manual for doing bad work at school?

- Read the first three chapters of the book, which set the scene and establish the characters of Joe and Chester. Do the children understand the 'Americanisms' that appear in the text? (This should not pose a problem since the American expressions are probably familiar to the children from television programmes and films.)

- What can the children tell you about Chester and Joe? Why do they think Chester is so difficult and rude? Do they think he will make friends? Why is Joe so hard on himself? (Great sensitivity must be shown here, not to draw attention to any particular child in the class who has special needs, nor to allow any of the children to use the opportunity to identify such children.) Explain that Joe finds difficulty with his class work and that Chester finds difficulty in settling into school and making friends. Ask the children to suggest why.

- Tell the children you are going to continue reading the book and they should look out for whether the two boys have changed by the end and, if they have, how they have changed. Remind them of what they said they thought the book might be about at the beginning of the lesson. How accurate were they in their predictions?

- Ask for a volunteer to explain how Joe and Chester felt at the start of the story and how they felt at the end. Through discussing the development of the story, help the children to realise that everybody has a difficulty to overcome but that everybody has a talent or a skill that can be developed. What did Chester's talent turn out to be? What was Joe's?

- Discuss what other issues could be raised in stories. Some examples are bullying, divorce, racism, green issues, religious intolerance and relationships. Do the children know of any books or stories that explore some of these issues? List these, and their subject matter, on a large sheet of paper and leave it for the children to refer to when choosing books. For example, *The Angel of Nitshill Road* by Anne Fine (bullying), *Brother Eagle, Sister Sly* by Susan Jeffers (the exploitation of Native Americans), *The Suitcase Kid* by Jacqueline Wilson (divorce), *Where the Forest Meets the Sea* by Jeannie Baker (conservation) and *Giant* by Juliet and Charles Snape (pollution).

With the lower-achievers

With adult support
Choose from:

1   Discuss the issues that were raised in the book. Explore some of the following ideas: Did Chester and Joe get on well at the beginning of the book? Why not? What was Chester's problem? What was Joe's? How did the two boys feel about themselves? Had their relationship changed by the end of the story? How? Did the boys feel better about themselves at the end of the book? How? What was Chester good at? What was Joe good at? Explain again to the group that everybody has a difficulty to overcome and that everybody has a talent or a skill that can be developed.

2   Help the children to complete Resource sheet 11a. Give reading support where necessary.

3   Discuss other social and moral issues with the children. Remind them of the topics suggested in the whole-class session: bullying, divorce, racism, green issues, religious intolerance and relationships. If possible, read other texts together that raise some of these issues. Encourage the children to add the titles of their favourites to the list started in the whole class session.

Teacher-independent activities
Choose from:

1   Let the children complete Resource sheet 11a, working in pairs for support.

2   Ask the children to work in pairs to create a short play about Chester and Joe. They should remember to show what the boys' problems were at the beginning of the story and how they overcame these.

3   Ask the children to work in pairs to look through two or three stories that raise different

issues. Ask the children to write their favourite story on the class list. They should write a sentence about why it is their favourite ready to tell the others about it during the plenary session.

Plenary session

■   Ask some of the children who made up a role-play about Chester and Joe to give a class performance. Did they remember to show both the problems and the talents of the two boys?

■   Ask the children who explored stories that raise other issues to tell the class about their favourite book.

Lesson Two

Intended learning

■   To understand how grammar alters when statements and questions are reversed.

■   To use the chosen text as a basis for exploring this.

With the whole class

■   Write on the board 'It is' and 'Is it' (without punctuation). Ask for volunteers to read them and explain the difference between them. Make sure they point out how the subject and the verb are reversed. Ask if any of the children can tell you why this is. Explain that this happens when the question form is being used. Ask somebody to come and write in the full stop and the question mark.

■   Invite volunteers to come to the board and write a simple statement. You could start them off with examples such as 'I can', 'She has', 'There is' and so on. Ask other children to tell you what the question form is for each of the examples on the board ('Can I?', 'Has she?', 'Is there?') Let them come and write the questions themselves.

■   Ask the children for some questions, for example 'Will you?', 'Does he?', 'Can they?' and so on. Challenge some of the children to make statements from the questions. Let them write these up.

- Play a game where one child (or you) decides what they are to be, such as a tiger or a butterfly, but they don't tell anyone. The other children ask questions, such as 'Are you a big cat?' or 'Can you fly?' and eventually say 'Are you a tiger?' When they have made the correct guess they say 'You are a tiger.'

- Look through *How To Write Really Badly* for some questions. For example, '…is it?' (page 13), 'Would you mind?' (page 15), 'Shall I choose it?' (page 28), and so on. Ask the children to tell you what the statement form would be. ('It is', 'You would mind' and 'I shall choose it'.) Point out how the subject and verb are reversed in each example.

With the lower-achievers

With adult support

Choose from:

1 Prepare a set of cards, half with a simple statement (subject and verb only) written on each and half with a simple question. Play a game where the cards are mixed up and placed face down on the table. The children have to take a card, read it and tell you the reverse order. If they are correct they win a token. The winner is the child with the highest number of tokens at the end of the game.

2 Give the children copies of Resource sheet 11b. Help them to turn the questions into statements and vice versa.

3 Give the children copies of Generic sheet 9 (page 125). They should write underneath each picture the related statement and question. For example, 'They can skip' and 'Can they skip?'

Teacher-independent activities

Choose from:

1 Let the children complete Resource sheet 11b, working in pairs for support.

2 Give the children copies of Generic sheet 9 (page 125). They should write underneath each picture the related statement and question. For

example, 'They can skip' and 'Can they skip?' Let them use dictionaries if they would like to.

3 Prepare a set of cards, half with a simple statement (subject and verb only) and half with a simple question. Mix up the cards and place them on the table face down. Give the children a 'Snakes and Ladders' board and a counter each. Let them play a game where they take a card, read it and say the reverse order. If the others agree they move their counter two spaces along the board. If they come to a snake or a ladder, they go up it. The winner is the child who reaches the top first. (They don't come down if they reach the top of a snake.)

Plenary session

- What happens to the subject and verb of a sentence when it is turned into a question? Ask the children for some examples. Make sure everybody understands how the grammar changes.

- Ask children to come to the front and act out some of the statements and questions they have been working on. For example, one child says to the other 'Can you hop?' and the other child hops and says 'I can hop'.

Lesson Three

Intended learning

- To spell words by analogy to other known words.

- To use the chosen text as a basis for practising this.

With the whole class

- Write 'light' on the board. Challenge the children to come and write as many other words with the same group of letters (ight) as they can think of – 'fight', 'might', 'night', 'right', 'sight', 'tight', 'bright', 'fright' and so on.

- Ask for volunteers to highlight the 'ight' in each word, using a different colour. Explain that, by learning this 'anchor group' of letters, they are able to spell many other words within the same family.

■ Invite the children to give you an 'anchor group' with different letters, for example 'ain', 'one' or 'eal'. Ask them for words that belong to each letter group. You could start them off with 'train', 'bone' or 'steal'. Let them write these on the board themselves. Which anchor group has the highest number of words?

■ Read pages 47 and 48 of *How to Write Really Badly* and remind the children of Chester's cue for remembering 'ould' words. Ask them to write words in this group on the board, for example 'could', 'should' and 'would'. Do they think Chester's method is good? Why/why not?

With the lower-achievers

With adult support

Choose from:

1 Give the children copies of Generic sheet 10 (page 126). Help them to write words for each anchor group. (You could work with them to make up mnemonics for each group.) They should write one sentence for each group of words on the back of the sheet.

2 Prepare a set of cards with an anchor group written on the front and a value between 1 and 6 written on the back. Have at least two cards for each value. Provide the children with a dice and place the cards in their numbered piles. Play a game where the children have to throw the dice and then take a card from the pile with the value they threw. They should read the anchor group and then give you a word. If they are correct, they 'win' the points of their dice throw. Help them to keep a tally of their points. The winner is the child with the highest total.

3 Prepare Generic sheet 1 (page 117) with the first 'brick' of each row containing one anchor group. You could use the groups from the whole-class session. Help the children to fill each 'brick' on that row with a word from the anchor group.

Teacher-independent activities

Choose from:

1 Give the children copies of Generic sheet 10 (page 126) to complete. They should use dictionaries to help them write words with the same anchor group of letters inside the tail pieces of the kites.

2 Give the children copies of Resource sheet 11c to complete. They might like to work in pairs. Make sure they have rhyming dictionaries and/or ordinary dictionaries. You might need to read the sheet with them first.

3 Give the children copies of Generic sheet 4 (page 120) and ask them to find pairs of words to write inside the matching shoes. Each pair should have the same anchor group of letters.

Plenary session

■ Write a sample word on the board, highlighting the anchor group in a different colour. Ask different children to spell (orally) other words within the same family.

■ With the whole class, write an advertising jingle that uses one or two sets of anchor group letters. Try to make it rhyme!

■ Complete these sentences about *How to Write Really Badly*. Use the words in the box below.

write   difficult   good   spell   draw   pictures
make models   read   make friends   play football

Joe couldn't _____

Chester couldn't _____

Joe helped Chester to _____

Chester helped Joe to _____

Everybody finds something _____ to do.

Everybody is _____ at something.

■ Now draw a picture and write about yourself.

I am good at _____

_____

I find it difficult to _____

_____

Name _____

■ Turn these into questions.

?

I can.→

It is.↘

There is.→

¿ _____

¿

←It will.

←You do.

.?

She has.→ _____

?

? ? ?

■ Turn these into statements.

Can it? → _____

Are there? → _____

Will they? → _____

Did you? →

Has he? ↗

Can we? → _____

■ Look at this advertising jingle. It has some words missing.
Choose some words from the box to help you complete it.

bright	fight	tight	might	night	light	sight

It's time to get it right!
It's time your teeth were _____!
Those germs you have to _____!
So clean your teeth at _____!

■ Now finish this jingle by finding your own words.
Use a dictionary to help you.

This latest pizza is such a **WOW**!
You'll want to go and buy one _____!
It's big and crusty and ever so yummy
Just wait until it's inside your _____!
Then you'll be screaming 'I WANT MORE!'
So don't waste time; get out that _____
And race to us at Pizza Place.
Everyone says that we are _____!

Stories from other cultures

Overall aims

- To explore stories from India in relation to the settings and content.

- To identify commas, semicolons and colons, and to understand their use.

- To use dictionaries when having to refer to the second and subsequent letters of a word.

Featured book

Tiger Roars, Eagle Soars by Ruskin Bond (Walker Books, 1994)

Story synopses

The book comprises two stories set in India. One is of a majestic old tiger and the other of a fierce and powerful eagle.

In the first story, when hard times come, the tiger is driven to kill the village buffalo. The villagers have to hunt it and two boys, Nandu and Chottu, reluctantly join in.

In the second story, the eagle hunts Jai's lambs and the young boy has to bravely defend his flock against the strong and powerful talons of the bird. The struggle ends with Jai winning, but only after an exciting and frightening encounter.

Lesson One

Intended learning

- To understand how settings influence events and incidents in the featured text and how they affect the characters' behaviour.

- To use the text as a basis to study other aspects of Indian culture.

- To be stimulated to discover other texts from different cultures for further study.

With the whole class

- Show the cover of *Tiger Roars, Eagle Soars* to the children (hide the title at first) and ask them where they think the stories might come from.

List their suggestions on the board. Discuss some of the following ideas about the cover: Does the illustration suggest that the stories are set in a city? How can you tell? Does it look like British countryside? What is different? What does the title suggest? Is it likely to be about British animals? Why not?

- Tell the children that the stories are set in India. Look at the list written at the beginning of the session. Had anybody guessed that the story was set in India? How did they know? Look at an atlas or globe. Where is India? Trace the distance from Britain.

- Read the opening line of *Tigers Forever*. Ask the children to tell you how this sets the scene in India. Why would it be impossible for this story to be set in Britain? Read the rest of the story.

- Discuss the elements in the story that are obviously Indian. For example, the names of the places and the people, the animals mentioned (the tiger, the buffalo and so on), the jobs done by the villagers, the environment, the temple and the clothing.

- Read the first two pages of *The Eyes of the Eagle*. Ask the children how they know this story is set in India. Could it also be a story about Britain? How do they know? Read the rest of the story.

- Again, discuss the Indian elements in the story. Write these on the board beside the list from *Tigers Forever*. What aspects are similar? What is different? Which story is their favourite? Why?

With the lower-achievers

With adult support

Choose from:

1   Discuss the two stories together. Why were Nandu and Chottu reluctant to join the tiger hunt? Do the children think the ending was a good one? Why or why not? Do they think that Jai was brave or foolish? Encourage them to give reasons for their answers. Ask the children to imagine they are Nandu, Chottu or Jai. Would they have done the same thing as the boys in the stories? Why or why not? Help the children to write a sentence or two beginning 'If I was ..., I would ...'

2 Using Resource sheet 12a, help the children to complete the sentences about the stories.

3 Provide the children with books about India and Indian culture. Explore together some of the aspects that are referred to in the book – for example, Hinduism, the climate, the fauna and the environment, the agrarian lifestyle and so on. Help the children to write and illustrate a book about India. Leave it on display for others in the class to read.

4 Explore together some books about other cultures, for example Native American, Chinese, Arab, Russian and so on. Encourage the children to make comparisons of aspects such as costume, food, housing, religion, physical geography and so on.

Teacher-independent activities
Choose from:

1 Let the children work in pairs to complete Resource sheet 12a.

2 Ask the children to draw a picture of either Nandu and Chottu and the tiger, or Jai and the eagle. Encourage them to write some sentences about their picture.

3 Prepare some A4 sheets divided into four sections, headed 'House', 'Clothes', 'Animals' and 'Food'. Ask the children to work in pairs to explore a book about another culture. They could choose India or a different culture. Ask them to illustrate each section on the sheet and write an accompanying caption.

Plenary session

■ Has anybody discovered something new about Indian culture since the whole-class session? Encourage them to tell the others about it.

■ If there are children in the class of Indian background, ask them to share some of their experiences and customs with the other children. Invite some of the Indian parents to come to school and cook some easily-prepared food such as samosa or bhajees.

■ Is anyone able to tell the class about a completely different culture from that of India?

Lesson Two

Intended learning

■ To identify commas, semicolons and colons, and to understand their use.

■ To use the featured text as a basis for exploring the use of this punctuation.

■ To find other texts and identify where the punctuation is used.

With the whole class

■ Before the lesson collect a few items such as a book, a ball, a pen, a tin and a ruler. You will also need an additional text with examples of colons.

■ Ask for a volunteer to draw on the board a comma. Ask the others if they agree this is what a comma looks like. What are they used for? Agree that they are used for lists or pauses.

■ Now draw on the board a colon and tell the children its name. Write 'colon' on the board. Explain that this is mostly used for introducing lists or ideas. Write on the board the following – 'I went to the shops and I bought: an apple, a banana, a carrot'. Stop there and ask the children what you have done. Agree that you have written a list using a colon to introduce the list and commas in the list itself. Leave this on the board for reference during the lesson.

■ Show the children the collection of items you gathered before the session and ask a volunteer to come to the board and write the names. Make sure they remember to put a comma after each item. Ask the children to suggest how the list might finish (with 'and' before the final item). Write above the list, 'These things are in my collection' and ask the children what punctuation is needed. Ask somebody to come and put in the colon after 'collection'.

■ Now draw a semicolon on the board and tell the children its name. Write the name alongside. Explain that semicolons are used to link main ideas or make larger divisions in lists. For example, 'The children couldn't go out to play; the snow was nearly a metre deep,' or 'For a new baby you will need a pram, a cot and bottles; nappies, sleepsuits and warm woollies.'

■ Together look through *Tiger Roars, Eagle Soars* for examples of commas and semicolons. (There are no colons in the text. Use other texts for this.) Look at the first line of *Tigers Forever* for commas, where extra information about the Ganges has been inserted. Page 6 has several examples of lists; page 60 has examples of pauses during reading. There are examples of how main ideas are linked with semicolons on pages 41, 54, 78 and 79.

With the lower-achievers

With adult support

Choose from:

1 Working closely with the children, look through some other texts for examples of commas, semicolons and colons. Discuss how each example is used and make sure the children fully understand the function of each punctuation mark. Help them to write a shopping list using commas, with an introduction and colon before it. Help them to link two sentences with a semicolon. For example, 'I wrote my shopping list; I can go to town now.'

2 Give the children copies of Resource sheet 12b. They should insert the correct punctuation marks in the sentences. Give reading support if necessary.

3 Write on the board 'I went to the shops and I bought:' and play the game with the group. As each child adds something to the list, write it on the board with a comma. Let them have a go at writing their own words.

Teacher-independent activities

Choose from:

1 Give the children copies of Resource sheet 12b to complete.

2 Have prepared some noun cards and several cards with a comma drawn on each one. Ask the group to play 'I went to the shops and I bought' They take a card from the noun card pile, lay it on the table and lay a comma card

after it, making a long line of objects and commas as they go. At the end they should work together to write out the list, starting with the words 'I went to the shops and I bought:' which should still be written up on the board from the whole-class session. Together they should agree the names and spellings of the objects in the list. They can use dictionaries to help them.

Plenary session

■ Ask for volunteers to come out and draw the punctuation marks. Ask other children what they are used for.

■ Together write some sample lists and sentences showing how the punctuation is used. These could be based on the two stories.

Lesson Three

Intended learning

■ To use dictionaries when having to refer to the second and subsequent letters of a word.

■ To use the featured text to practise using dictionaries.

■ To be able to use dictionaries when working with other texts.

With the whole class

■ Write on the board some names that begin with the same letter and that the children would recognise. If possible, use the children's own family names, as they will be familiar with their registration order. Use a different colour to highlight the second letter of the names and explain to the children that they should use these letters to put the names into alphabetical order. Go on to show the class how we use the third and fourth letters to put words in alphabetical order as well.

■ Write on the board a selection of words that begin with the same letter but have different second letters. Challenge the children to place these in alphabetical order. Do the same where the first two/three/four letters are the same.

■ Look again at the words you wrote on the board. Ask for volunteers to look for these in the dictionary and find the definitions. Make sure everybody understands how words are listed. Spend a little more time practising, using the dictionary if necessary.

With the lower-achievers

With adult support

Choose from:

1 Choose five or six words from *Tiger Roars, Eagle Soars* beginning with the same letter but with different second letters. Write them on the board and ask the children to put them into alphabetical order. Together, look them up in the dictionary and read the definitions. Show the children how the words in a dictionary are listed.

2 Give the children copies of Resource sheet 12c. Help them to put the words into alphabetical order. Then ask them to find the second set of words in the dictionary and write the definitions. Give support if necessary.

3 On Generic sheet 4 (page 120), write words in the shoes on the left-hand side of the page, such as 'balloon', 'clothes', 'garden', 'morning' and 'window'. Challenge the children to use dictionaries to find a second word for each which begins with the same letter but where the second letter of the words means that the word comes after the first word in the dictionary. For example, 'brother', 'coming', 'great', 'much' and 'work'.

Teacher-independent activities

Choose from:

1 Give the children copies of Resource sheet 12c to complete.

2 On Generic sheet 11 (page 127), write some words beginning with the same letter in the boxes, such as 'above', 'across', 'almost', 'along', 'also', 'always' and so on. Ask the children to work in pairs to find the words in a dictionary and write their definitions alongside.

3 Prepare several sets of cards (three cards in each set). The cards in each set should have a word beginning with the same letter but with different second letters (take them from a class dictionary). Ask the children to sort the cards into order and then stick them on the wall with sticky tack. Ask them to find the words in the dictionary and write the definitions on separate slips of paper. Encourage them to stick the definitions beside the appropriate words. Leave the words and their definitions on display while working on this lesson.

Plenary session

■ Ask the children who made the wall display to explain to the others what they had to do. Make sure they talk about using the second letter of the words to look them up. Take the word cards down and give them out. Challenge the children to put them back up in order.

■ Ask somebody to name a letter of the alphabet. Then ask four or five volunteers to write on the board words beginning with that letter. Challenge someone to put the words in order by writing numbers next to them. Invite other children to find the definitions in the dictionary.

Name _____

■ Read 'Tiger Roars, Eagle Soars'.

■ Put a tick (✓) in the 'Yes' or 'No' box.

Are the stories set in Britain? Yes ☐ No ☐

Are there wild buffaloes in India? Yes ☐ No ☐

Would you see a wild tiger in Britain? Yes ☐ No ☐

Do some eagles live in India? Yes ☐ No ☐

■ Finish these sentences. Use the words in the box to help you.

Chottu, Nandu and Jai lived in _____

Chottu and Nandu helped to hunt a _____

The tiger had killed the village _____

Jai's job was to look after the _____

An _____ tried to take a lamb.

Jai was scared but he was very _____ too.

| Britain | lion | buffalo | lambs | brave |
| India | eagle | coward | mountain | tiger |

■ Draw these punctuation marks.

colon	comma	semicolon

■ Name these punctuation marks.

 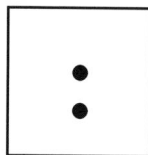 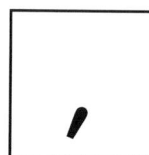

_____ _____ _____

■ Write the correct punctuation in these sentences.

It was raining ☐ we couldn't go out.

This is what's in my bag ☐ two pens ☐ some keys and some money.

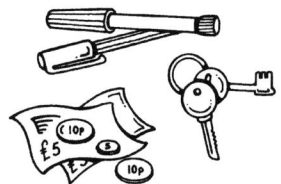

Today it's very cold ☐ it will snow tomorrow.

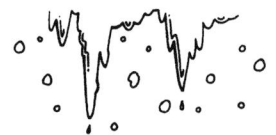

Here's Mum's shopping list ☐ six eggs, three apples ☐ four bananas and some milk.

a b c d e f g h i j k l m n o p q r s t u v w x y z

■ Use the alphabet to put these words in order.

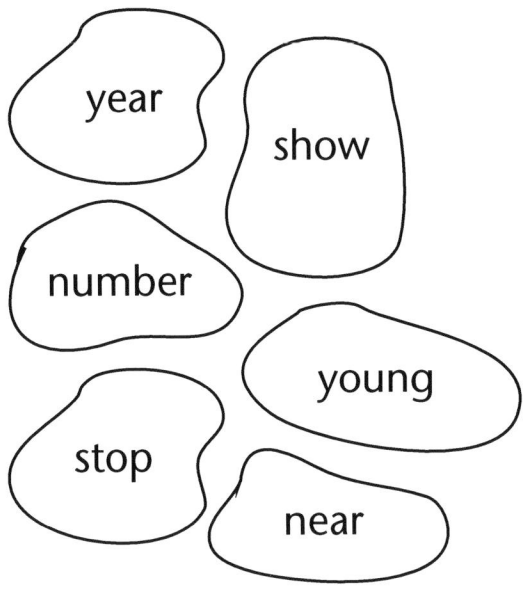

year

show

number

young

stop

near

1 _____

2 _____

3 _____

4 _____

5 _____

6 _____

■ Look in the dictionary for these words and write what they mean.

fry _____

fly _____

spin _____

skin _____

■ Choose three of the words above and write sentences for them on the back of this sheet.

Stories with chapters

Overall aims

- To understand how chapters are used to build up ideas and move the narrative forward.
- To identify and understand the use of dashes.
- To distinguish the two forms 'its' (possessive) and 'it's' (contraction).

Featured book

Dolphin Boy by Julie Bertagna (Mammoth, 1999)

Story synopsis

Amy's brother Dibs cannot speak. He creates havoc both at school and at home and Amy often feels extremely angry that her brother is not like other boys she knows. One day, they find a stranded baby dolphin on the beach. It is taken to the Sealife Sanctuary and, over the following weeks, Dibs bonds with the dolphin. He helps it to communicate in dolphin clicks and whirrs, without realising that it helps him to begin communicating with his family. By the time the dolphin is released into the wild, Dibs and Amy have also formed a bond that brings happiness to the whole family.

Lesson One

Intended learning

- To use the text to identify chapters.
- To understand how chapters are used to set the scene, build up ideas and move the narrative forward.

With the whole class

This lesson will take several sessions.

- Show the title page of *Dolphin Boy* to the children and ask what they think the story might be about. Can they guess what a 'dolphin boy' might be? Do they think this story might be fantasy, adventure, science fiction or 'real life'?
- Look at the contents page with the children and point out the two columns of numbers

separated by titles. Ask the children what this page is for. What does each set of numbers mean? What are the titles?

- Write 'chapter' on the board. Ask for a volunteer to explain what it means. Tell the children that chapters are used to set the scene of a book, to build up the ideas in the story, to move it forward and to make the reader want to read to the next stage. Often a chapter ends with a 'cliffhanger'. Write these ideas on the board and leave them up.
- Point to the numbered columns on the contents page. Ask the children what they are. Tell them that the numbers in the first column are the chapter numbers and the second column of numbers shows the page number of a chapter's beginning. Do the children know what the titles between the two sets of numbers are? Explain that they are the chapter titles.
- Read the first chapter of *Dolphin Boy*. At the end, ask the children whether the story has finished. How do they know? Agree that the end of the chapter has left the reader wanting to go onto the next part of the story. What do they think will happen next? What else has the opening chapter done? The children should know, for example, that it has introduced the setting, the characters and the characters' feelings.
- Read the rest of *Dolphin Boy*. At the end of each chapter, discuss how the narrative has moved the story forward and how the cliffhangers are created.

With the lower-achievers

With adult support

Choose from:

1 Make sure that the children fully understand the term 'chapter' and why chapters are used. If necessary, use other texts to explore again how chapters correspond to the given page number on the contents page. Look at the opening and ending of each chapter of *Dolphin Boy* and discuss each stage of the story. Encourage the children to identify the cliffhangers and them momentum of the action from chapter to chapter.

2 Give the children copies of Resource sheet 13a. Help them to complete the chart about Chapter 1 in *Dolphin Boy*. The idea is that they will see how a chapter sets the scene and how the ending can be used to make them want to read the next chapter.

3 Let the children choose some familiar and favourite books that have chapters. Together, explore how the chapters set the scene of the story, move the story forward and tempt the reader to move on to the next stage by ending on a cliffhanger. It is likely that the children have not considered favourite stories in these terms before, so using well-known books is a good way of exploring these ideas.

Teacher-independent activities

Choose from:

1 Ask the children to work in pairs to choose one or two favourite and well-known books which have chapters. (Provide a selection at a suitable reading level rather than give them a free hand in the library.) They should write the chapter numbers and titles and make notes about what happens in the chapter and how it leaves the reader. For example, 'At the end of Chapter 2, I want to know if the dog dies.'

2 Give the children copies of Resource sheet 13a to complete. You may need to go through one example with them first before letting them work independently.

3 Ask the children, in pairs, to write two or three sentences about whether or not they liked the chapter endings in *Dolphin Boy*, saying why.

Plenary session

Before the session, cover the functions of chapters that were written in the whole-class session.

■ Ask the children who looked at other books to tell the rest of the class what they found about the chapters. Invite them to read their résumés of the books' chapters.

■ Ask for some volunteers to tell everybody why books have chapters. Uncover the list from the whole-class session. Were all the functions of a chapter mentioned?

Lesson Two

Intended learning

■ To identify and understand the use of dashes.

■ To explore the chosen text for dashes.

With the whole class

■ Draw a single dash and a pair of dashes on the board and ask the children if they know what they are. Can they tell you what they are used for? Explain that the single dash is used mainly to show an afterthought to the idea in the main sentence. Write an example on the board, such as 'You can't go out to play – it's pouring with rain.' Ask for some other examples. Let the children come and write them on the board.

■ Tell the children that double dashes are usually used to replace parentheses or brackets. Explain that they are also used for afterthoughts or additions to the main idea in a sentence, but in the middle of the sentence rather than at the end. For example, 'The team lost the match – they didn't score any goals – so they weren't very happy.' Point out that without the phrase in parenthesis, the main sentence still makes sense. Ask the children for some more examples. Let them come and write them on the board.

■ Show the children examples of dashes in *Dolphin Boy* (pages 36, 44, 58, 77). Read the paragraph containing the dash, making an obvious pause at the dash for emphasis.

With the lower-achievers

With adult support

Choose from:

1 Make sure the children understand why dashes are used, both singly and in pairs. Together, decide on some examples for both types. Help the children to write these to share in the plenary session.

2 Using Resource sheet 13b, help the children to put the dashes in the appropriate places. Can they make up an example for a single dash and a double dash? They could write these on the back of the sheet.

Teacher-independent activities

Choose from:

1 Give the children copies of Resource sheet 13b to complete, working in pairs to support each other.

2 Prepare a set of cards with dashes on each one, and a set of cards with related sentences, one sentence per card. For example, card 1 says, 'The team lost the match', card 2 says, 'they didn't score any goals' and card 3 says, 'so they weren't very happy.' (Be careful with the punctuation.) The children should put the cards together, with the dashes, and then write the sentences they make.

Plenary session

■ Ask the children who wrote some sentences using dashes to read their work. Let them show the others their writing and point out the dashes. Encourage them to explain why they used dashes.

■ Does everybody understand why dashes are used? Is there anything they find difficult about dashes?

Lesson Three

Intended learning

■ To distinguish the two forms 'its' (possessive) and 'it's' (contraction).

■ To use these correctly in own writing.

With the whole class

■ Write on the board some examples of well-known contractions such as 'I can't go out', 'He's very good' and 'You've got to come.' Ask

the children to explain why you have used an apostrophe and what the full words would be. ('I cannot go out', 'He is very good' and 'You have got to come.')

■ Point to 'He's very good'. Ask someone to come out and write out the other third person singular forms. ('She's' and 'It's') Can somebody else come out and write the full form? ('She is' and 'It is') Using a different colour, highlight 'It's' and ask for examples of sentences using 'It's'. You could start the children off with, 'It's cold today' or 'It's not funny'.

■ It is possible that one of the children will suggest an example using the possessive, such as 'The dog ate its dinner', written as 'The dog ate it's dinner'. Use the opportunity to explain that we do not use an apostrophe in this case. Point to the 'It's' and 'It is' examples and ask the children whether 'The dog ate it is dinner' makes sense.

■ Play a game of 'Its It's Football'. Divide the class into two 'football' teams (with the children's choice of names!) and appoint a 'goalkeeper'. Ask 'players' from each team in turn to say whether or not an apostrophe is used in your verbal sentence. For example, *"Adam, does 'The cat cleaned its whiskers' need an apostrophe?"* or *"Lee-Wei, does 'In summer it's hot' need an apostrophe?"* If the child answers correctly, they score a goal. Keep the game to three or four minutes and make sure you ask each side the same number of questions.

With the lower-achievers

With adult support

Choose from:

1 Make sure the children fully understand that 'it's' is a contraction of 'it is' and that 'its' is the possessive of 'it'. If necessary, explore a few more examples together. Write them on the board with a gap where 'it's' or 'its' should be. Ask the children to finish them. If they make mistakes, reassure them and let them rub out the errors and try again.

2 Give the children copies of Resource sheet 13c. Help them to insert 'it's' or 'its' in the sentences. Give reading support where necessary. They

should then put a tick or a cross beside the sentences at the bottom of the sheet.

3 Have prepared some cards with 'it's' written on them and some with 'its'. Each child in the group needs one of each. Call out sentences with 'it's' or 'its' in them. The children have to decide which version is correct and hold that card up for you to see. The advantage here is that the other children won't see if someone is wrong and it will encourage them all to take part without fear of being wrong.

Teacher-independent activities

Choose from:

1 Give the children copies of Resource sheet 13c to complete. You may need to read it to them first. If necessary, let them work together in pairs for support.

2 Prepare a set of cards with a sentence on each. The word 'it's' or 'its' should be missing. Make sure there are examples of both sorts. Ask the children to write the sentences inserting the correct form.

3 Prepare two sets of cards, one with 'it's' or 'its' written on each card, and one with a sentence minus 'it's' or 'its'. Make sure there is the same number of cards in each set. The children should play a game where the sentence cards are placed face down on the table. The children take one, read it and take a correct card from the other pile. If the others agree they are right, they win a token. They should then put the sentence card to the bottom of the pile. The winner is the child with the highest number of tokens at the end of the game.

4 Prepare a set of cards with a sentence on each, to include either 'its' or 'it's'. Place the cards face down on the table. Give the children a 'Ludo' board and some tiddlywinks. They should play a game where Child A takes a card and reads it to Child B who decides whether there should be 'its' or 'it's' in the sentence. If Child B is correct, they move their tiddlywink five spaces around the board. Child B then takes a card and reads it to Child C, and so on. The winner is the child who reaches the centre of the board first.

Plenary session

■ Ask the children who played games to explain the rules to the others. Let them read some of the sentence cards aloud. Ask them to tell you when 'its' or 'it's' should be used.

■ What did the children enjoy about this lesson? Do they all understand when to use 'it's' or 'its'? Use a few examples once more to check.

■ Think about Chapter 1 of *Dolphin Boy*.
Now complete these sentences.
The words in the box below will help you.

The main characters are _____

_____

The chapter is set in _____

and _____

Dibs is unusual because _____

_____

Amy feels _____ and _____

because of Dibs.

Amy	Dibs	speak	jealous	school
draw	angry	love	home	clever
beautiful		upset	proud	bedroom

■ Now finish this sentence.

I did/did not want to know what happened next because

_____

_____

_____

■ Look at these sentences with dashes.

You can't go out to play – it's pouring with rain.

The team lost the match – they didn't score any goals – so they weren't happy.

■ Put dashes into these sentences.

The cat ran up a tree a dog was chasing it.

I told the dog whose name was Buster to stop barking.

We went to the beach instead of the swimming pool for a swimming lesson.

I ate four chocolate biscuits I was very hungry.

■ It's means 'It is'. Its means 'something that it owns'.
Put **it's** or **its** in these sentences.

The dog licked _____ paws.

Today _____ very hot weather.

We like poetry because _____ fun to read.

The bird laid _____ eggs in _____ nest.

Dad's car lost _____ wheels.

_____ cold in the winter.

■ Put a tick (✓) beside the right sentences and a cross (✗)
beside the wrong ones.

My cat washed its whiskers. ☐

It's too wet to go out. ☐

The dog ate it's bone. ☐

You can't do that – it's not fair. ☐

I'm going by bus – its too far to walk. ☐

The baby wanted it's dinner. ☐

Poems and poetical terms – 1

Overall aims

- To revise, understand and use correctly the poetical terms 'rhyme', 'rhythm' and 'alliteration'.

- To identify examples of these in poetry.

- To use the chosen poems as a basis for own work.

Featured books

Another Second Poetry Book compiled by John Foster (Oxford University Press, 1988)

A Third Poetry Book compiled by John Foster (Oxford University Press, 1982)

Lesson One

Chosen poems

'Huff' by Wendy Cope, page 104

'Wellie Weather' by Jacqueline Brown, page 104

Intended learning

- To revise, understand and use correctly the poetical terms 'rhyme' and 'rhythm'.

- To explore these in the chosen poetry.

With the whole class

- Enlarge copies of 'Huff' and 'Wellie Weather'. Read 'Huff' with the children, letting them follow the text. Ask them what the poem is about. Do they understand the feelings of the child in the poem? Why or why not?

- Ask them to think about the rhyme in the poem. What does 'rhyme' mean? Ask a child to come out and point to the rhyming words ('bad'/'had', 'year'/'fear', 'amends'/'friends' and so on). Ask the children to identify the rhyming pattern of the poem (the second and fourth lines rhyme). Remind them of the work they did on this in Chapter 10.

- Ask the children what rhythm means. If necessary, recite some nursery rhymes together,

gently clapping the rhythms as a reminder. Encourage them to join in clapping the rhythms. Continue to practise this until the children are confident in what they are doing.

- Read 'Huff' again, clapping out the rhythm. Ask the children to tell you what the rhythm is (four beats and three beats, on alternate lines). Read the poem together once more, encouraging the children to clap the rhythm themselves.

- Read 'Wellie Weather' with the children, encouraging them to follow the text. Invite them to tell you what the poem is about. Ask them to look carefully and find the rhyming words. If necessary, show them that the rhyming words appear just before the end of each line: 'pane days'/'-vane days'/'-blain days', 'away days'/'clay days'/'play days' and so on.

- Read the poem again, gently clapping out the rhythm. Ask the children to tell you what the rhythm is (four beats and then two beats in the final line). Read the poem once more, encouraging the children to gently clap the rhythm themselves.

With the lower-achievers

With adult support

Choose from:

1   Give an enlarged copy of 'Wellie Weather' to the group. Explore the poem together and help the children to find the rhyming words. Let them draw circles around each set of rhyming words, using different colours for each set. Together, clap out the rhythm again. Ask the children to tell you what the rhythm is (four beats and two beats in the final line). Do the same with 'Huff', using an enlarged copy to identify the rhyming words. What is the rhythm (four beats and three beats, on alternate lines)?

2   Give the children copies of Resource sheet 14a. Help them to identify the rhyming words. Let them draw circles around each set of rhyming words, using different colours for each set. Ask them to recite the nursery rhyme, clapping the rhythm and writing in the boxes the number of beats in each line.

3   Give the children a copy of another rhyming poem. Help them to identify the rhymes in the poem and circle them in different colours. Challenge them to identify the rhythm in each line. Let them write at the end of each line the number of beats it has.

4   Help the children to practise reciting a verse from one of the poems, clapping the rhythm as they speak. Tell them they will have the chance to give a class performance during the plenary session.

Teacher-independent activities

Choose from:

1   Give the children copies of Resource sheet 14a to complete.

2   Give the children copies of Generic sheet 1 (page 117). They should write the rhyming words from the poems in the 'bricks'.

3   Ask the children to write their favourite verse from either 'Huff' or 'Wellie Weather' and illustrate it with an appropriate border. They should write each rhyming word in a different colour and then write at the end of each line the number of beats it has.

Plenary session

■   Let the children who practised reciting a verse and clapping its rhythm give a class performance. Ask them to do a repeat performance encouraging the others to join in.

■   Choose another poem or part of a poem and write it on the board (the poems on pages 30, 75 or 76 in this book will be suitable). Together read the poem and ask the children to tell you the rhyming words. Ask someone to come and circle them. Then together count the number of beats in each line and write them at the end. Does everyone agree?

Lesson Two

Chosen poems

'A little alliteration' by Mike Jubb, page 105

'Cottage' by Eleanor Farjeon, page 105

Intended learning

■   To understand and use correctly the poetical term 'alliteration'.

■   To explore this in the chosen poetry.

■   To use the chosen poems as a basis for own work.

With the whole class

■   Enlarge copies of 'A little alliteration' and 'Cottage'.

■   Write on the board the word 'alliteration'. Ask the children to tell you what it says. Do they know what it means? Remind them of the work they did on alliterative patterns during Year 2. Give them a few starter examples, such as 'slimy, slithering slugs' or 'great, greedy gorillas'. Then ask them to give you some more examples.

■   Use some of the children's names in an alliterative phrase. For example, 'Gentle Jack juggled with giant jellies' or 'Super Susan slithered swiftly in the snow'. (Be sensitive to the children's feelings, using both alliterations that are positive and children who will not mind being used as an illustration.)

■   Read 'A little alliteration', letting the children follow the text. Ask them to identify the alliterations. Let them come out and point to each one on the enlarged copy. Explore some of the words together, for example 'lizards' and 'liquorice', 'snortsomeful' and 'snickerish'. Which are real words? Which are nonsense words? Do the children like these words? Encourage them to say why or why not.

■   Read 'Cottage' to the children, letting them follow the text. Ask for volunteers to come out and point to each example of alliteration. Explain that this poem is much older than 'A little alliteration', so we can see that alliteration has been used by poets for a very long time.

With the lower-achievers

With adult support

Choose from:

1 Make sure the children fully understand what 'alliteration' means. Make up some alliterative sentences using the names of pop stars or sportspeople. Help the children to write some of these down.

2 Give the children copies of Resource sheet 14b. Help them to match each half of the alliterative lines. Warn them to look and listen carefully for One and Eight. Challenge them to make up a line of alliteration using the initial letter of their first name.

3 Allocate a line of 'A little alliteration' to individual children. Help them to practise reciting the poem for a class performance, using intonation and emphasis to help express the alliterations in an interesting way.

4 Using Resource sheet 14c, help the children to match the lines to either 'rhyme' or 'alliteration'.

Teacher-independent activities

Choose from:

1 Give the children copies of Resource sheet 14b to complete. They should work on this in pairs for support. You may need to read it through with them first. They may not make the connection with 'One' and 'wiggling' and 'Eight' and 'aching' so this will need explaining to them. The explanation will clarify the rest of the task.

2 Write out for the children the two phrases 'lizards licking liquorice' and 'children chewing chocolate chips'. Say that their task is to write another phrase (or more) for each phrase, leaving the verb in the phrase but finding new alliterative nouns. For example, 'lions licking lollies'.

3 Let the children complete Resource sheet 14c. Again they may need to work in pairs for support and you may need to read the sheet through with them first.

Plenary session

■ Ask the children who practised 'A little alliteration' to give a class performance.

■ As a class make up an alliterative poem. It doesn't have to rhyme. It could be based on the children's names, for example 'Andy's amazing ant, Bernard's big bunch of bluebells' and so on.

■ Teach the children a tongue-twister, such as 'Peter Piper...'

Huff

I am in a tremendous huff –
Really, really bad.
It isn't any ordinary huff –
It's one of the best I've had.

I plan to keep it for a month
Or maybe for a year
And you needn't think you can make
      me smile
Or talk to you. No fear.

I can do without you and her and
      them –
Too late to make amends.
I'll think deep thoughts on my own
      for a while,
Then find some better friends.

And they'll be wise and kind and
      good
And bright enough to see
That they should behave with proper
      respect
Towards somebody like me.

I do love being in a huff –
Cold fury is so heady.
I've been like this for half an hour
And I feel better already.

Perhaps I'll give them another chance,
Now I'm feeling stronger,
But they'd better watch out – my
      next big huff
Could last much, much, much longer.

Wendy Cope

Wellie Weather

Steamed-up rainy pane days
Twirling weather-vane days
Red-hot fingered chilblain days –
      Wellie weather.

Icy underfoot days
Snow transformed to soot days
All mothers' scold and tut days –
      Wellie weather.

Shivering stray cat days
'Don't forget your hat!' days
Nice children turned to brats days –
      Wellie weather.

Half the class away days
Games-field turned to clay days
Indoor dinner-time play days –
      Wellie weather.

Gas-fire turned up to three days
Scalding-hot soup for tea days
Watching far too much TV days –
      Wellie weather!

Jacqueline Brown

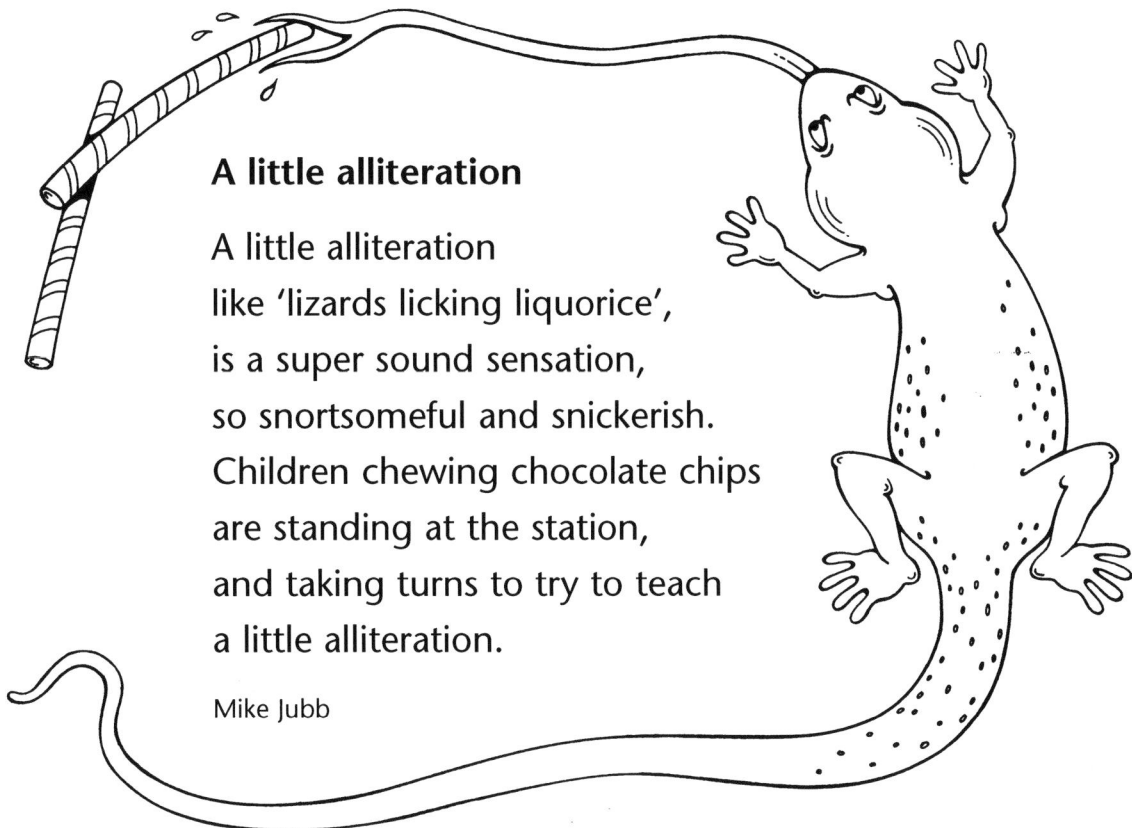

A little alliteration

A little alliteration
like 'lizards licking liquorice',
is a super sound sensation,
so snortsomeful and snickerish.
Children chewing chocolate chips
are standing at the station,
and taking turns to try to teach
a little alliteration.

Mike Jubb

Cottage

When I live in a Cottage
I shall keep in my Cottage

Two different Dogs,
Three creamy Cows,
Four giddy Goats,
Five pewter Pots,
Six silver Spoons,
Seven busy Beehives,
Eight ancient Appletrees,
Nine red Rosebushes,
Ten teeming Teapots,
Eleven chirping Chickens,
Twelve cosy Cats with their Kittenish Kittens
    and
One blessed Baby in a Basket.

That's what I'll have when I live in my Cottage.

Eleanor Farjeon

Name _____

■ Circle the words that rhyme. Use a different colour for each set.

day   tea   clay   fly

shy   play   three   see   try

■ Write the sets here.

■ Read this rhyme aloud and write in the boxes the number of beats in each line.

One, two, three, four, five ☐ beats
Once I caught a fish alive ☐ beats
Six, seven, eight, nine, ten ☐ beats
Then I let it go again. ☐ beats

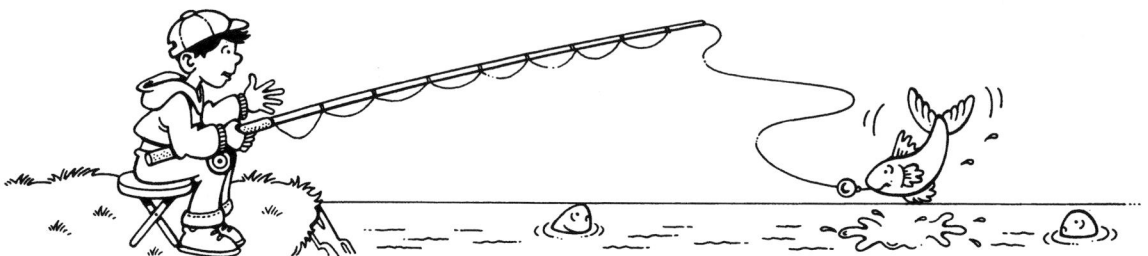

■ Match the halves to make lines of alliteration.
Be careful with the first one – listen carefully to
the sound of the words!

One	throbbing thumbs
Two	sizzling sausages
Three	aching angels
Four	wiggling worm
Five	nice nurses
Six	tootling tractors
Seven	ticklish tigers
Eight	funny farmers
Nine	forgetful fools
Ten	steaming soups

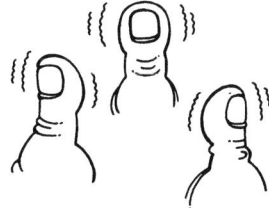

■ Write a line of alliteration for the initial letter
of your first name.

_____

■ Read these and match them to 'rhyme' or 'alliteration'.

Five fat frogs flopping in the foam.

rhyme   alliteration

Sammy wants to jump up high
Until he reaches to the sky.

rhyme   alliteration

Patsy ate up all the cake,
Now she has a tummy ache.

rhyme   alliteration

Henry the hedgehog hurried home,
Happy in his hedgehog heaven.

rhyme   alliteration

Poems and poetical terms – 2

Overall aims

- To understand and use correctly the poetical terms 'verse', 'stanza', 'couplet' and 'chorus'.
- To identify examples of these in poetry.

Featured books

A Spider Bought a Bicycle and other poems for young children selected by Michael Rosen (Kingfisher Books, 1987)

THERE'S AN AWFUL LOT OF WEIRDOS IN OUR NEIGHBOURHOOD by Colin McNaughton (Walker Books, 1987)

Lesson One

Chosen poems

'Little by Little' by Michael Rosen, page 112

'I HAVE NEVER BEEN SO HAPPY' by Colin McNaughton, page 112

Intended learning

- To understand and use correctly the poetical terms 'verse' and 'stanza'.
- To explore these in the chosen poetry.

With the whole class

- Enlarge copies of 'Little by Little' and 'I HAVE NEVER BEEN SO HAPPY'.
- Tell the children they are going to explore verses and stanzas in these poems. Read 'Little by Little' with them, letting them follow the text. Ask them what they think the poem is about. Do they know what 'verse' means? Remind them that it is a section of a poem, usually written in lines. How many verses are in 'Little by Little'? Encourage them to identify a rhyme pattern. (They shouldn't be able to, since there isn't one.) Is there a regular rhythm? (No) Explain that because there aren't any regular patterns of rhyme or rhythm, the poem has verses, not stanzas.

- Tell the children you are going to explore the next poem and decide together whether it has verses or stanzas. Read 'I HAVE NEVER BEEN SO HAPPY' to them, letting them follow the text. Do they find this poem funny? Encourage them to give reasons for their responses. Challenge them to identify the rhyme pattern. (Three consecutive rhyming lines, followed by a fourth non-rhyming line.) Ask them to tell you the rhythm pattern. (Four beats in three lines and three beats in the final line.) Are these patterns regular in all the verses? Explain that because they are regular patterns of rhyme and rhythm, the verses are called 'stanzas'. Make sure they understand that the rhyme or rhythm of a poem has to follow a regular pattern for it to have stanzas.

With the lower-achievers

With adult support

Choose from:

1 Explore both poems again, making sure the children understand the difference between verses and stanzas. Discuss together the regular rhyme and rhythm patterns of the stanzas in 'I HAVE NEVER BEEN SO HAPPY'. Help the children to see that 'Little by Little' has no regular rhyme or rhythm in its verses.

2 Help the children to complete the sentences on Resource sheet 15a. Give reading support if necessary.

3 Look at some other poetry together and help the children to identify whether it has verses or stanzas. (Nursery rhymes are a good source of stanzas and modern poetry often has verses.) Together you could list the poems under the headings 'has stanzas' and 'has verses'.

Teacher-independent activities

Choose from:

1 Let the children complete Resource sheet 15a.

2 Give the children a sheet of A4 paper divided in two and headed 'has verses' and 'has stanzas'. Ask them to work in pairs to look at other poems and rhymes. They should decide whether the poems and rhymes have verses or

stanzas and write the names of the poems in the appropriate columns.

3   Ask the children to draw a large picture to illustrate one of the verses or stanzas of either poem. They should write a caption to say whether the poem has verses or stanzas.

Plenary session

■   Ask for volunteers to tell you what a verse and a stanza are.

■   Did some of the children find other examples of poetry with verses and stanzas? Ask them to tell the others about the poems they explored.

■   Let the children who drew illustrations of one of the featured poems talk about their picture and read the accompanying caption.

Lesson Two

Chosen poems

'MONDAY'S CHILD IS RED AND SPOTTY' by Colin McNaughton, page 113

'Johnny's So Long at the Fair' (traditional), page 113

Intended learning

■   To understand and use correctly the poetical terms 'couplet' and 'chorus'.

■   To explore these in the chosen poetry.

With the whole class

If possible, have a copy of the traditional verse, 'Monday's Child', available.

■   Enlarge copies of 'MONDAY'S CHILD IS RED AND SPOTTY' and 'Johnny's So Long at the Fair'.

■   Tell the children that they are going to learn about couplets and chorus in these poems.

■   Read 'MONDAY'S CHILD IS RED AND SPOTTY', letting the children follow the text. Explain that the poem is a parody of the traditional rhyme, 'Monday's child'. If possible, read this to the children as well.

■   Tell the children that a 'couplet' consists of two consecutive lines of rhyme, usually the same length. Look again at the poem and ask the children to identify the couplets. Let them come and point out the rhyming words in each couplet ('spotty'/'potty', 'bed'/'fed', 'toys'/'noise' and 'day'/'OK').

■   Explain that a chorus is part of a poem or song that is repeated after each verse. Originally, people listening to the poem or song would join in with the chorus.

■   Read 'Johnny's So Long at the Fair', letting the children follow the text. Ask the children what the poem is about. Encourage them to identify the chorus of the poem. Read the poem again, encouraging them to join in with the chorus.

■   Ask the children for other examples of poems or songs with a chorus – for example, 'This Old Man'.

With the lower-achievers

With adult support
Choose from:

1   Read 'MONDAY'S CHILD IS RED AND SPOTTY' again, pausing at the end of each line and encouraging the children to supply the rhyming couplets. Give out copies of Generic sheet 4 (page 120) and ask the children to write the rhyming words in the pairs of shoes. Read 'Johnny's So Long at the Fair', encouraging the children to join in the chorus at the appropriate places. Help them to learn the chorus for a class performance.

2   Give the children copies of Resource sheet 15b. They should choose the correct word to make rhyming couplets in the poem.

3   Using Resource sheet 15c, help the children to fill in the missing words.

Teacher-independent activities
Choose from:

1   Let the children complete Resource sheet 15b.

2   Ask the children to work in pairs and find other poems with couplets (nursery rhymes are a good source). Give out copies of Generic sheet

4 (page 120) and ask them to write the rhyming words from the couplets in the pairs of shoes.

3   Let the children work in pairs to complete Resource sheet 15c.

Plenary session

- Ask children who completed resource or generic sheets to explain to the class what their task was. Encourage the children to use the terms 'couplet' and 'chorus' in their talks.

- Ask for volunteers to tell you what 'couplet' and 'chorus' mean. Does everybody understand what they have been working on during this lesson?

Little by Little

In England they say:
Little drops of water
make the mighty ocean.

In France they say:
Little by little
the bird makes his nest.

In Spain they say:
Little by little
the cup is filled.

In Japan they say:
Dust can pile up
to make a mountain.

In Arabic people say:
A hair from here
and a hair from there
makes a beard.

In Germany they say:
Many drops of water
dripping onto a stone
can make a hole in it.

Michael Rosen

I HAVE NEVER BEEN SO HAPPY

I have never been so happy
Since my dear old mom and
    pappy
Packed the car and left real
    snappy,
Said they'd had enough.

I can eat just what I feel like,
Make up any kind of meal, like
Mars bars, chips and jellied eels,
    like
Mommy never made.

To nursery school I gave up
    going,
They teach you nothing that's
    worth knowing,
And anyway there's movies
    showing
In the afternoons.

And bedtime, well, it's up to me
    now,
Midnight, two or half past three
    now.
Sometimes I'll just watch TV now
All night long.

So if you're listening, mom and
    pappy,
As you can see I'm really happy,
But could you come and change
    my nappy,
Mommy, Pappy, please!

Colin McNaughton

MONDAY'S CHILD IS RED AND SPOTTY

Monday's child is red and spotty,
Tuesday's child won't use the potty.
Wednesday's child won't go to bed,
Thursday's child will not be fed.
Friday's child breaks all his toys,
Saturday's child makes an awful noise.
And the child that's born on the seventh day
Is a pain in the neck like the rest, OK!

Colin McNaughton

Johnny's So Long at the Fair

(CHORUS)   Oh dear, what can the matter be?
Oh dear, what can the matter be?
Oh dear, what can the matter be?
Johnny's so long at the fair.

He promised to buy me a bunch of blue ribbons,
He promised to buy me a bunch of blue ribbons,
He promised to buy me a bunch of blue ribbons,
To tie up my bonny brown hair.
CHORUS: Oh dear, what can the matter be? etc

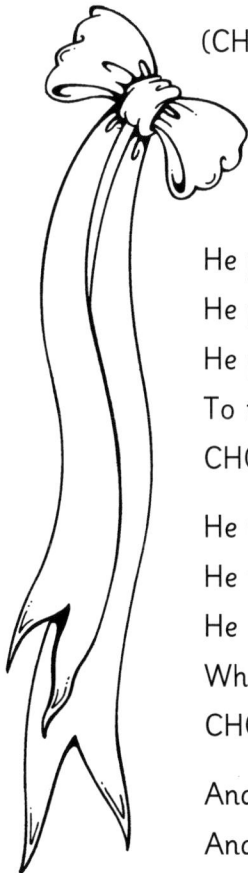

He promised to buy me a fair ring would please me,
He promised to buy me a fair ring would please me,
He promised to buy me a fair ring would please me,
When he had gone to the fair.
CHORUS: Oh dear, what can the matter be? etc

And then for a kiss, oh he vowed he would tease me,
And then for a kiss, oh he vowed he would tease me,
And then for a kiss, oh he vowed he would tease me,
When he had come home from the fair.
CHORUS: Oh dear, what can the matter be? etc

Name _____

■ Look for the poetical words in the wordsearch.

r	a	r	l	e	s	p
e	v	h	s	y	t	a
g	e	y	t	z	a	t
u	r	m	a	s	n	t
l	s	e	n	a	z	e
a	e	e	v	r	a	r
r	h	y	t	h	m	n

verse

stanza

rhyme

rhythm

pattern

regular

■ Put the words into the sentences.

A v_____ is part of a poem.

A poem doesn't have to _____

It doesn't need a regular _____

A _____ is also a verse.

It always has a _____ pattern of rhyme or rhythm.

■ Read the poem and choose the missing word from the boxes.

A week's verse of children

Monday's child is a horrible brat,

Tuesday's child sits on the _____

| cat |
| dog |

Wednesday's child has a runny nose,

Thursday's child sucks his _____

| ears |
| toes |

Friday's child does things in his nappy

Saturday's child is cross and _____

| funny |
| snappy |

But Sunday's child, from what I've seen

Is just as horrible, bad and _____

| sweet |
| mean |

Collette Drifte

■ Recite the first stanza of 'This Old Man'.

■ Now read the lines below and the labels.

> This old man, he played two,
> He played knick-knack on my shoe 〉 stanza

> With a knick-knack Paddywack.
> Give a dog a bone,
> This old man came rolling home. 〉 chorus

■ Fill in the missing words.

> This old man, he played _____
> He played knick-knack on my _____
>
> | three |
> | knee |
>
> 〉 _couplet_

> With a knick-knack Paddywack.
> Give a dog a bone,
> This old man came rolling home. 〉 _____

> This old man, he played _____
> He played knick-knack on my _____
>
> | four |
> | door |
>
> 〉 _____

> With a knick-knack Paddywack.
> Give _____
> This _____ came rolling home. 〉 _____

Story planner

Title of story

Period of time story is set in

Setting where story takes place

Characters in the story

Story beginning

Story middle

Story ending

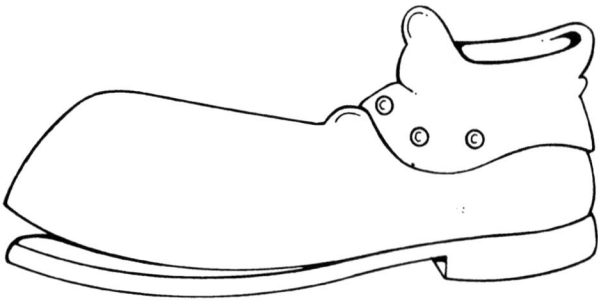
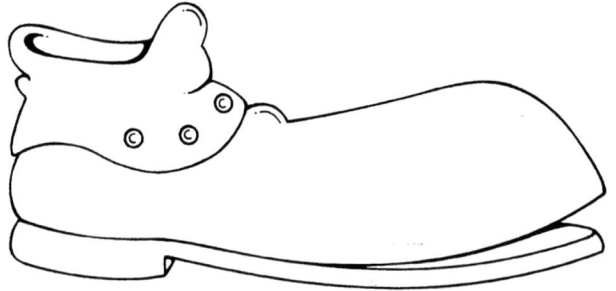

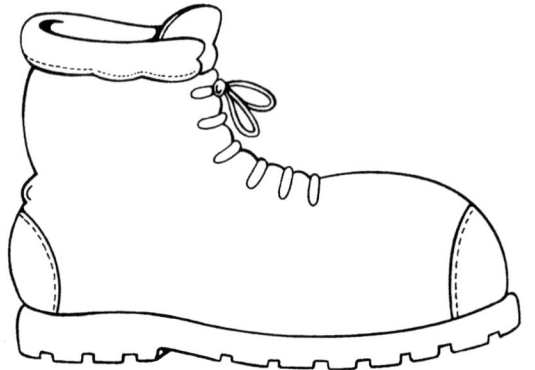
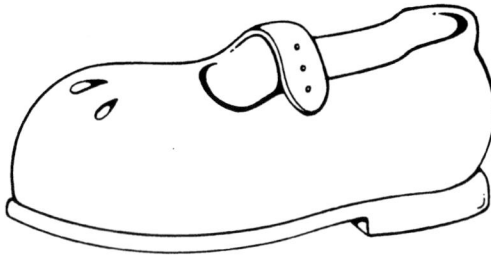
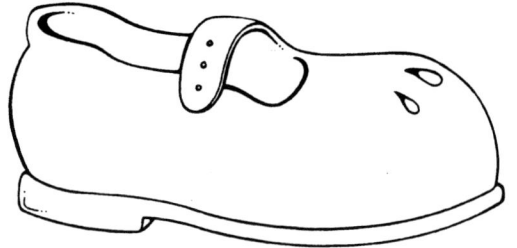
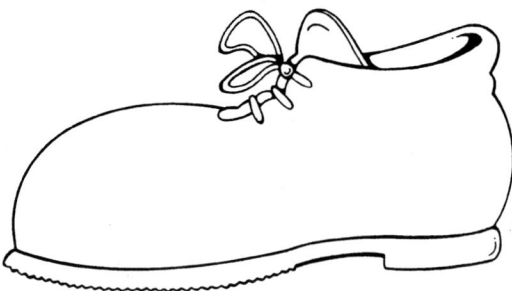
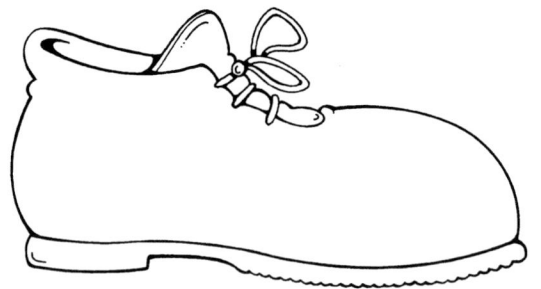

■ Finish these sentences about the series of books you have read. Use the words at the bottom of the sheet to help you.

_____ is a series of books about

_____

The characters in the books are all _____

_____

The stories have a _____ ending.

They are set in _____

_____

| same | happy | present | Britain |
| sad | past | abroad | different |

■ Look at these words.

interest ⟶ interesting ⟶ interested

■ Can you make new words from these?

write → _____ → _____

dark → _____ → _____

long → _____ → _____

drive → _____ → _____

play → _____ → _____

run → _____ → _____

sad → _____ → _____

duck	drake	goose	gander
fox	vixen	prince	princess
lion	lioness	tiger	tigress
actor	actress	brother	sister
mother	father	grandmother	grandfather

Fantasy stories

	Jack and the Beanstalk		
Fantasy setting			
Fantasy characters			
Fantasy events			

_____
_____

_____
_____

_____
_____

_____
_____

_____
_____

_____
_____

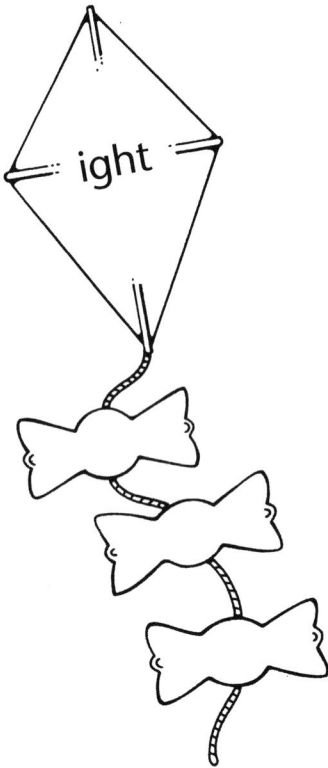

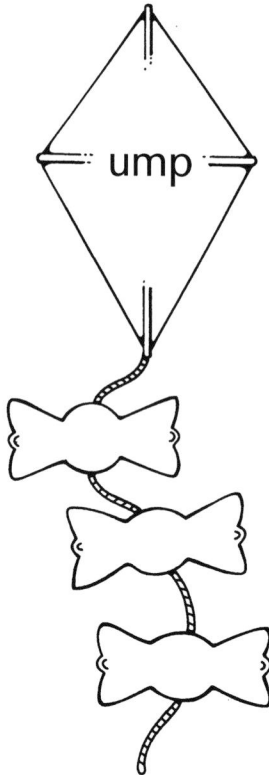

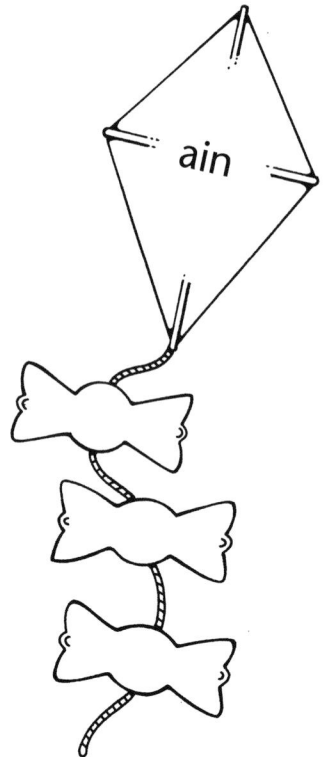

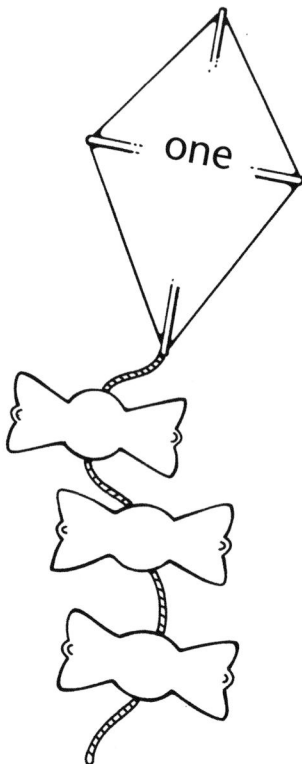

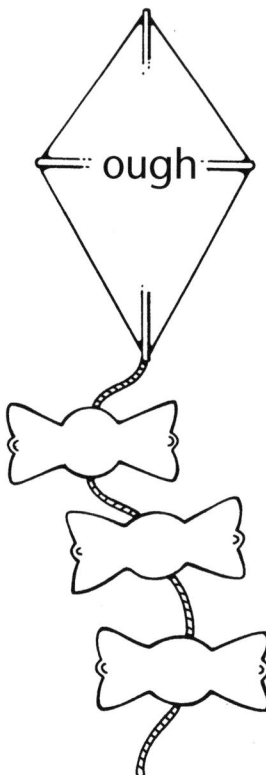

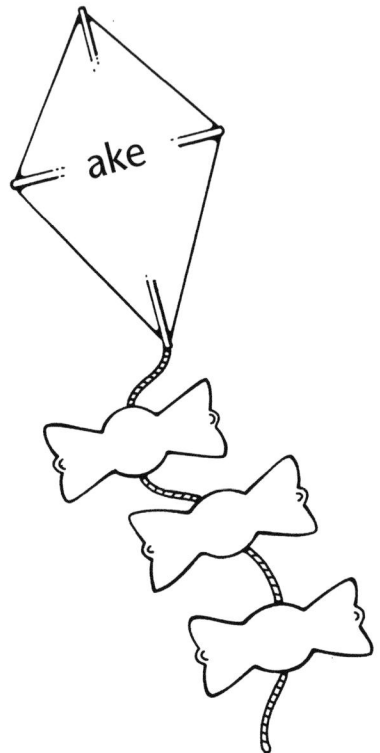

■ Look for these words in the dictionary and write what they mean.